Super Natural Cooking

# Super Natural Cooking

**FIVE WAYS TO INCORPORATE
WHOLE AND NATURAL
INGREDIENTS INTO
YOUR COOKING**

Heidi Swanson

**CELESTIAL ARTS**
**Berkeley | Toronto**

Celestial Arts
an imprint of Ten Speed Press
P.O. Box 7123
Berkeley, California 94707
www.tenspeed.com

Distributed in Australia by Simon and Schuster Australia, in Canada by Ten Speed
Press Canada, in New Zealand by Southern Publishers Group, in South Africa by
Real Books, and in the United Kingdom and Europe by Publishers Group UK.

Cover and text design by Toni Tajima

Library of Congress Cataloging-in-Publication Data
Swanson, Heidi, 1973–
        Super natural cooking : five delicious ways to incorporate whole and
natural foods into your cooking / by Heidi Swanson.
            p. cm.
Includes bibliographical references and index.
ISBN-13: 978-1-58761-275-6 (pbk.)
ISBN-10: 1-58761-275-5 (pbk.)
1. Cookery (Natural foods) I. Title.
TX741.S887 2007
641.5′63—dc22                      2006030536

Printed in China

First printing, 2007

4 5 6 7 8 9 10 — 11 10 09 08 07

# CONTENTS

# ACKNOWLEDGMENTS

I don't think it's much of a stretch to say it takes a village to create a cookbook. For this one, it was certainly the case. First I want to thank Wayne. Not everyone would put up with the endless pile of dishes that goes along with the creation of a book like this. He was always game for a quick trip to the store if I was short an ingredient or two (even if it was cold and raining out) and was never thrifty with his opinions or support. You mean everything to me, and I hope everyday that we will continue to enjoy a long life of wonderful adventures (and delicious meals) together.

To Aaron, Lorena, and my dream team at Ten Speed Press for championing this book from the start, I couldn't have hoped for a better collaboration. Special thanks to Lily Binns and Meghan Keeffe for your insight, direction, editing skills, and most importantly, for being fantastic sounding boards. Toni Tajima, what can I say? It was my lucky day when she took on the design of this book. I can't think of anyone I'd rather trust with taking my photography and text from the pixel realm to the printed page. To Jasmine Star, Carolyn Miller, and Ken DellaPenta, a big thanks as well. And to the small army of friends and family who tested (and retested) countless recipes and helped out in so many other ways. Your palates and point of views helped shape every recipe you see here: Lulu LaMer, Brian Sharp, Gary and Janelle Swanson, Heather and Mark Ruder, Shay Curley, Lanha Hong-Porretta, Gwen McGill, Whitney Moss, Quyen Nguyen, Shauna James, Yong Cho, Jen Luan, Veronica Benda, Sejal Hingrajia, Steve Sando, Bruce Cole, Katherine and Janet McCartney, Mary Lou Bremser, Heather Flett, Ross O'Dwyer, Brette Luck, Amanda Berne, Molly Stevens, Reina Perez, and Milla Koukkunen.

# INTRODUCTION

There is a natural foods co-op as big as a football field located in the heart of San Francisco just a short distance from my house. Clear plastic bins stretch down row after row, holding a seemingly impossible array of salts, dried seaweeds, bulk flours, heritage beans, colorful grains, and a kaleidoscope of spices. The containers start at my toes and reach skyward toward the rafters.

The beans sit at eye level and tempt me with their beautiful patterned skins. One aisle away, the palette of flours ranges in color from pristine white to sandy brown and in texture from powder-fine to rough and raggy tiny flakes. Fresh tortillas steam up their plastic bags to my right, and a huge bin of preserved lemons brightens up one of the refrigerator displays.

On one hand, being in a store like this can be exciting, but if you aren't prepared, it can be downright intimidating. Faced with a dozen different types of dried seaweed, the flood of questions hits hard: Do some variations taste more sealike than others? What about the different textures? Which seaweeds are particularly salty, or fishy, or fragrant, and do you always rehydrate them, or do you sometimes use them dry? If so, when? And so it goes as you begin to explore and cook with the bounty of under-utilized whole ingredients.

Like me, many of you probably grew up on standard American fare—flour was all-purpose, and sugar more often than not was white granulated. Not to start this book off on a sour note, but there is a lot of room for improvement when it comes to the ingredients found in the average American pantry. A common snapshot would include commercially raised fruits and vegetables of dubious origin, industrially produced cooking oils, highly refined sugars, and nutritionally barren flour. Before these products made their way into your house or apartment, many were showered with agricultural chemicals, treated with chemical solvents, and stripped of most of their vitamins, minerals, fiber, and flavor.

The good news is the growing availability of whole foods from farmers' markets, CSAs, independent natural foods stores, food co-ops, and stores like the rapidly expanding Whole Foods Markets. It is getting easier each day to find sources for whole foods, and part of the fun and excitement is in the discovery. This discovery and exploration of ingredients is a big part of what I write about on my websites, the recipe journal 101cookbooks.com and the whole-foods-focused MightyFoods.com.

I am excited about sharing with you much of what I know about cooking with whole, natural, minimally processed ingredients, along with some of my favorite recipes. You can start swapping out heavily processed ingredients with more healthful (and better-tasting) ones, many of which are outlined in the first chapter of this book, "Build a Natural Foods Pantry." If I suspect an ingredient might be tricky to locate, I'll offer up alternate suggestions for more readily available ingredients you might substitute.

I encourage you to think about how your cooking could change if you entirely eliminated ingredients like all-purpose white flour, white sugar, and other highly processed ingredients. I hope this book will convince you that a whole world of exciting flavors and nutritionally rich ingredients will be there to greet you. Once you have the swing of it, shopping for and cooking with these ingredients isn't any harder and doesn't have to take more time than what you are already used to. There are quick and easy recipes alongside more intensive undertakings (if you really want to go for it), as well as fresh twists on everyday favorites, like polenta made from the tiny teff grain, barley-based risotto, or trans-fat-free thin mint cookies.

# *The Spirit of the Term* Natural

The word *natural* is one of the most abused terms in food marketing. Consumers will pay up to 30 percent more for products labeled "natural," even though there are no regulations concerning which products (outside of meat and poultry) can be labeled as such. As a result, you can end up with groceries in your cart that you think are healthful, but are actually laden with high-fructose corn syrup and hydrogenated oils.

The term *natural* is open to interpretation, but here is what it means to me: Natural ingredients are whole—straight from the plant or animal—or they are made from whole ingredients, with as little processing and as few added flavorings, stabilizers, and preservatives as possible, thus keeping nutrients and original flavors intact; for example, tomatoes crushed into tomato sauce, cream paddled into butter, olives pressed into olive oil, or wheat berries ground into flour. For me, focusing on natural ingredients also means avoiding genetically modified and chemically fertilized crops, as well as dairy products that come from cows treated with growth hormones. Take these natural foods with their super-nutritional profiles, their unique and complex flavors, and their lighter impact on the environment and you have an expansive and exciting realm to explore—*Super Natural Cooking*.

Many make the argument that our bodies find it easier to utilize the whole foods our species has been consuming for thousands of years. The body doesn't even recognize as food some of the modern highly processed products and convenience foods that have been introduced into the food supply in the last sixty years. And worse, some of these new "foods" are actually highly damaging, trans fats being an excellent case in point. Volumes have been written about this, as well as the way many of the diseases we are seeing in epidemic proportions (diabetes, heart disease, certain cancers) were nearly nonexistent in many cultures subsisting on a diet of local, all-natural foods—even when their primary fat was a saturated fat, like that found in coconut oil. It wasn't until a refined Western diet was adopted by these cultures that incidents of these (now common) diseases spiked.

This book will be your guide to navigating a less-processed, more natural world of cooking ingredients. Instead of making you feel limited by taking away ingredients from your cooking repertoire, when you are finished with this book I hope you will find yourself inspired by all the possibilities and techniques you can explore within this rich culinary palette.

This can be a complicated realm to navigate, and during those times when my brain goes to mush browsing the fourteen different flours in front of me, or I'm confused by a new oil that just hit the market, I've found that I can typically figure out what fits into my definition of a natural ingredient by asking myself two questions: If pressed, could I make this in my own kitchen? And, can I explain how this is made to an eight-year-old? I'm looking for two *yes* answers here.

# The Recipes

I chose my favorite everyday-type recipes to share in this book. They were selected with the aim of showing you how versatile, delicious, and unintimidating a diet of natural and whole foods can be. The recipes will introduce you to some new ingredients, help you feel comfortable with them, and hopefully inspire more experimentation on your part over time.

The recipes are vegetarian, though many lend themselves to a wide range of adaptations. Many people think a vegetarian diet is healthier—and it certainly can be—but be aware that vegetarian fare is subject to the same issues we've already talked about. As with so-called natural foods, many products marketed to vegetarians may be laden with unhealthful ingredients. A particular problem is many of the meat substitutes, which can be packed with preservatives, artificial flavors, and genetically modified soy. Again, the key is to seek out foods in as close to their natural state as possible.

This book is divided into five main chapters. For starters, you will learn how to take a critical look at your own pantry. Beyond that, you will find four recipe-driven chapters clustered around specific ideas—exploring whole grains, cooking by color, understanding how to identify and utilize superfoods, and using a range of natural sweeteners. It is hard to choose favorites, but for those of you who feel like you are treading into unchartered territory, take a stab at the Toasted Wheat Germ Soup on page 54, the Curried Tofu Scramble on page 90, the Sprouted Garbanzo Burgers on page 155, or the Seed-Crusted Amaranth Biscuits on page 36. These recipes come together quickly and utilize easy-to-find ingredients.

# chapter one

# Build a Natural Foods Pantry

# BUILD A NATURAL FOODS PANTRY

This chapter aims to set you up with something other than the standard powder-white pantry. It's a whole new (and at the same time old) way of thinking about cooking from scratch.

When cookbooks repeatedly call for the familiar cast of cheap, refined, basic ingredients, people forget how to use anything else. The ingredients they seldom use fall out of favor, and they lose confidence in experimenting with new ones. Many of the ingredients that have fallen out of favor with the home cook are whole grains and whole-grain flours, natural sweeteners, and minimally processed fats.

The ingredients outlined here are going to be your building blocks—your go-to pantry of culinary fats, flavors, and flours. This doesn't mean you have to take what you are currently using and throw it out, it just means that the next time you head to the store you will be armed with the information (and hopefully inspiration) to choose differently.

Just because you overhaul your pantry it doesn't mean that you have to banish your favorite family recipes. Cook enough of the recipes in this book and you'll be able to do updated versions of your favorites using better-quality (and better-tasting) ingredients.

Use this chapter as a shopping primer. The focus here is on what to buy, what to look for, and how to navigate toward more healthful ingredients. You will encounter more information on grains and sweeteners (as well as info on other ingredients) in chapters 2 through 5, with more of an emphasis on how to cook and prepare them.

## *Flours, Meals, and Powdery Stuff*

When you think of flour, chances are the first thing that comes to mind is the processed white variety known as all-purpose flour, created by stripping wheat berries of their nutrient-rich bran and germ prior to processing. It is then "enriched" by adding a small fraction of the original nutrients

back in so that the final product isn't completely devoid of nutrients. Baking recipes you are familiar with often call for this type of wheat flour.

The good news is that there is a whole spectrum of other flours out there that can be used in everything from savory main courses to sweet baked goods. Flour can be milled from grains other than wheat; it can also be milled from an exciting range of nuts and legumes. I've even seen banana and coconut flours.

One thing to keep in mind is that using alternative flours isn't always as simple as swapping one for another (although sometimes this is the case). Different flours have different properties, including gluten-protein levels, absorbency, appearance, texture, and of course flavor. The information in the front of this chapter will help you not only understand the recipes in this book, but help you make educated substitutions when you are working with recipes from other books as well.

We well know that different grains (as well as nuts and legumes) contain different types of protein and in varying amounts. So it follows that the many different kinds of flours contain different types of proteins. When it comes to baking however, the proteins that concern us are the ones found in wheat flour—the gluten-forming proteins, glutenin and gliadin. When these particular proteins come into contact with moisture and motion (kneading or beating), they produce gluten and this gluten forms a network lending structure and elasticity to dough. While all wheat flours contain some level of these gluten-proteins, the amounts vary. For instance, durham wheat, whole-wheat, and unbleached all-purpose flours (which are all milled from hard wheat) typically have gluten protein levels in the 12 to 14 percent range, while cake and pastry flours (milled from soft wheat) come in at around 7 to 10 percent. This is the reason hard wheat flours are the defacto choice for baking bread, making pasta, and creating super-stretchy pizza dough. If you are after a more tender crust, biscuit, cake or muffin, you are better off using a soft pastry flour. Wheat gluten is considered by some to be the only "true" gluten, but other nonwheat flours can contain some gluten as well. Typically, there is not enough to form the structure you get from wheat gluten, but enough to cause problems for people with gluten allergies.

I know it's confusing, but also keep in mind that flours can be nutritionally high in protein, but have no *gluten-forming* proteins, for example quinoa flour. It is important to make the distinction. Try to make a leavened bread using 100 percent quinoa flour, and you are destined for trouble.

As you'll see, I like to blend some of the low-/no-gluten-protein nonwheat flours with wheat flours. You end up with the structure you need from the gluten proteins in the wheat flour, alongside the interesting flavors, textures, and nutritional profiles that come with the nonwheat flours. I've also armed you with substitution tips on the following pages to help when you are working with recipes from other books.

## General Guidelines

The natural oils in whole-grain flours can go rancid quickly at room temperature, so purchase them from a store with high turnover. Refrigerate or freeze these flours as soon as you get home, or at least store them in a cool, dark place. In the refrigerator or freezer, store them in an airtight container so they don't pick up flavors from other foods and moisture. Flours that are bought in smaller amounts, for example from the bulk/bin section, can be refrigerated in wide-mouthed Mason jars. Flours that come in larger, multi-pound bags I normally seal in large, reusable plastic freezer bags. Also, look for stone-milled flours, which are ground slowly; this method doesn't generate the nutrient-compromising heat that occurs in other milling methods like hammer milling and roller milling.

What follows is by no means a comprehensive list of every possible flour; that could fill an entire volume in itself. Rather, think of this as a list of favorites.

## Wheat Flours

People are convinced that the minute you make something whole wheat it's destined to be brown, heavy, and unappetizing. This couldn't be further from the truth. Because there is a range of whole-wheat flours to choose from, the key to successful use is understanding which whole-wheat flour to use when. These are two of my go-to wheat flours.

WHOLE-WHEAT PASTRY FLOUR is a powdery flour made from soft red winter wheat or soft white winter wheat. Its lower gluten protein content (relative to standard whole-wheat flour) makes it great for recipes where you want a nice, tender crumb—quick breads, biscuits, muffins, cookies, and cakes. It can be substituted one-to-one for all-purpose white flour in many cases with good results. Using whole-wheat pastry flour instead of straight whole-wheat flour alleviates much of the heaviness often associated with whole-wheat baked goods. Of course, you would still opt for whole-wheat flour with its high gluten protein content if you were making a loaf of hearty artisan walnut bread, but this is a great flour to explore in all those recipes where you are after a nice crumb.

WHITE WHOLE-WHEAT FLOUR is also fantastic and can replace all-purpose white flour one to one. It is less heavy than traditional whole-wheat flour but more flavorful than all-purpose white flour. If you're trying to slip whole grains into your cooking under the radar, this is an ideal flour to turn to.

## Nonwheat Whole-Grain Flours

High in protein, AMARANTH FLOUR works well as an accent in combination with other flours. Because it's a New World ingredient ground from the tiny amaranth grain, I like to pair it with other New World foods, but broadly speaking it has a natural affinity for chiles, cheese, honey, corn, brown sugar, and seeds. Try the Seed-Crusted Amaranth Flour Biscuits on page 36 or you can start by substituting amaranth for up to one-fourth of the all-purpose flour called for in recipes for waffles, pancakes, quick breads, cookies, and muffins. Toasting can mellow its assertive flavor. Keep in mind that it has no wheat gluten. Pairing it with a wheat flour in recipes where a leavener is used (or needed) helps.

Mild and sweet, with malty undertones, BARLEY FLOUR lends itself nicely to baked goods. Although barley flour does contain some gluten, it's not enough to make a dough rise effectively and is often used in conjunction with a wheat flour. When using barley flour in baked goods, reduce the oven temperature by 25°F for more even baking. The maltiness lends itself nicely to pairing with lemon or other citrus fruits. Start by swapping it in for 25 to 50 percent of the flour in recipes, especially in breads, pancakes, crepes, and scones.

CORN FLOUR simply comes from grinding up dried corn. This flour lends vibrant color and sweet flavor to favorites like muffins, corn bread, crepes. Favor stone-ground whole-corn flour, and keep it refrigerated.

OAT FLOUR lends a moist, creamy sweetness to cookies, cakes, and piecrusts. For me, oats evoke a natural feeling of contentment. Maybe it's the warming spices they are traditionally prepared with, or maybe it's the memories of growing up with many cozy winter breakfasts enjoyed alongside my little sister. Either way, this comforting quality extends into food prepared with oat flour as well. Though there is no naturally occurring gluten in oats, low levels of gluten are detected in oat flour and evidently come from cross-contamination with other grains during milling and transport. Start by substituting up to 25 percent oat flour in quick breads, cakes, and muffins. It cozies up well with berries, seeds, and generous drizzles of honey.

The cross-contamination from other grains that adds gluten to oats can be a problem for some gluten-sensitive people; if you're on a gluten-free diet, you'll need to be careful about using oats, as well as other "nongluten" flours to be sure they'll work for you.

I discovered QUINOA FLOUR quite by accident when I couldn't find the buckwheat flour I was searching for at the time. Milled from a tiny, fiber-rich power grain, it has a soft texture and a grassy taste that becomes more tempered when cooked. I use it as the base of my favorite crepe recipe (page 48). While it has a high-protein content at 17 percent, it is gluten free, so combine it with a wheat flour for baked goods. As with many of the other flours in this section, start by substituting up to 25 percent. I like to pair it with corn, potatoes, chiles, pine nuts, and brown sugar. Like amaranth, it generally goes nicely with other New World ingredients.

Most of the TEFF FLOUR I've encountered comes from brown teff grains. (There is also ivory teff available if you want to grind it into an ivory flour.) An obscure, iron-rich mini grain indigenous to Ethiopia, the flavor and color of brown teff is rich and seductive to both the eye and the palate. Make a tart crust using 50 percent teff flour and you'll see what I mean— dark, sophisticated, and delicious. Teff is a gluten-free flour that excels in all sorts of applications—rustic quick breads, cookies, cakes, pie- and tart crusts, and even biscuits. Start by substituting a modest percentage of teff flour (25 percent), and go from there. It is possible to use a higher percentage of teff flour in a recipe with good results, particularly in nonleavened endeavors like tarts, or the teff polenta on page 58. You can also use the tiny whole grains of teff to thicken soups, stews, and sauces.

## Nongrain Flours and Meals

It may surprise you to learn that flours are sometimes made from foods other than cereal grains. But flour is basically a powder of varying fineness that can be made from any food, including nuts and vegetables.

A native of Russia, buckwheat is actually an herb, not a cereal grain. You've most likely had BUCKWHEAT FLOUR in the form of soba noodles or crepes. Although it's great for crepes and pastas, its purplish gray tone lends an odd shade to baked goods. It is low in gluten and has an affinity for buckwheat honey, ginger, and fruits on the tart side of sweet, like cherries, cranberries, and other berries.

If I can convince you to track down just one esoteric flour, MESQUITE FLOUR would be it, even though it can be hard to find. Also known as mesquite meal, this flour made is made from the ground pods of the mesquite tree. It has a scent that is warm and comforting, but without the edge of warm spices, such as cinnamon or even cinnamon's mellower Mexican cousin, canela. When heated, mesquite flour permeates the kitchen with a mellow, sweet fragrance. Because it lacks gluten, start by substituting about 25 percent mesquite flour in place of regular flour in baked goods. Because of its distinct, slightly sweet, malty, smoky flavor, it also works beautifully as an everyday seasoning. Sprinkle it over oatmeal, add it to banana-based smoothies, or dust it over piping hot corn bread. It can be a bit pricey, but the amount needed to make an impact on most recipes isn't much. (See Sources for mail-order suppliers.)

My favorite pancakes use WILD RICE FLOUR as their secret ingredient (page 43). As I explain in the chapter on grains, wild rice isn't technically a grain at all; because it is used like one though, I squeezed it in there anyway. It is a marsh grass native to North America. Wild rice flour is more difficult to locate than whole-grain wild rice, and if you can't find a source for it, grind your own in small batches until powder fine using an electric coffee or spice grinder. Start by substituting this rich, textured, hearty gluten-free flour for 25 percent of the all-purpose flour in recipes.

## Flours to Avoid

It is important to stay away from commercially processed flours that contain bleaching agents and chemical additives; instead, opt for pure flours made from whole, intact (preferably organic) ingredients.

# Oils and Fats

If you look in the average American pantry or refrigerator, you are likely to see a relatively small range of oils and fats used for cooking and food preparation. Everyone has their favorites: Canola oil, butter, margarine, peanut oil, and olive oil are all common. Coconut oil and pistachio oil? Not so common. Navigating the world of oils and fats can be confusing, and the learning curve is challenging. The good news is that you have a lot more choice these days—a range of flavors, a range of smoking points, and a range of nutritional benefits. Each of these aspects varies in relation to the individual oil or fat and how it is processed. The best fats and oils are the ones that are carefully produced and handled to retain their natural flavor and beneficial nutritional components.

Simply put, oils are produced by pressing oil-rich foods until they release their fluids—olives, nuts, seeds, and coconut are all used in this way. What happens after this point is a crapshoot and really depends on the producer. Butter, on the other hand, is produced differently. Maybe when you were a kid someone gave you a small jar full of cream with a marble in it and told you to shake. Remember how, after ten long minutes of shaking, the jar would contain a small gem of butter? The liquid sloshing around outside of the butter? Buttermilk. It makes sense, right? Unfortunately, not all production of commercial cooking oils is as straightforward.

The amount of information and misinformation surrounding fats is overwhelming. What you need to keep in mind is this: At the end of the day, fat plays an essential role in overall health and well-being. We all need to consume moderate amounts of healthy fats to maintain optimal health. Fats help keep the body insulated and protect vital organs. Fat-soluble vitamins use dietary fats to make themselves bioavailable to the body. Also keep in mind that how you use fats in cooking impacts the texture and flavor of the food immensely. Choosing the most beneficial fat to enhance or complement a recipe can be exciting once you clear a few basic informational hurdles.

For starters, not all fats and oils are produced equally. The nutritional content of heavily refined oils can be hugely compromised during commercial processing. High temperatures, solvents, deodorizing, and chemical defoamers are all problems. If maintaining the nutritional properties in the food you cook is important to you, be diligent about seeking out high-quality unrefined oils made from organic ingredients. Not all oils get check marks in both categories, but aim high nonetheless. Organic is important, because pesticides and other toxins tend to collect and concentrate in the fatty portion of the plant. Look for unrefined and expeller-pressed oils so you know the final product is as nutritionally intact as possible. These methods ensure that important but fragile components like essential fatty acids, carotenes, and chlorophyll are preserved to the greatest extent possible as the oil makes its journey from the farm to your table.

Assuming you purchase a good-quality oil, you want to make sure its quality isn't diminished once it enters your home. Just as high heat can damage oils during processing, exposure to heat and light can degrade oils during storage. It's important to refrigerate many oils, especially once they're opened. Ideally, they'd be stored in dark or opaque glass containers, too. Some oils, particularly those rich in omega-3 fatty acids, should never be heated, but this isn't a problem, as there are many others that do well at higher temperatures.

Use your nose as a first line of defense. If oils ever smell rancid or "off," toss them out. Buy top-quality oils, store them carefully, and heat them only to the point where they are fragrant. Refined oils that tout sky-high smoking points can do so because they've been stripped of nutritionally beneficial components that contribute to a lower smoking point.

Many unrefined oils are also rich in beneficial essential fatty acids (EFAs)—nutritionally necessary fatty acids that the body cannot produce on its own and that must be obtained through dietary sources.

There are three different kinds of fats: saturated, monounsaturated, and polyunsaturated. Most oils are composed of a combination of these, but often one type will predominate. Saturated fats are typically solid at room temperature; coconut oil and butter fall into this category. Olive oil is the most commonly used type of monounsaturated fat, a type of fat that's liquid at room temperature but thickens when chilled. Polyunsaturated fats remain liquid even when chilled; oils from flaxseeds, hemp seeds, pumpkin seeds, canola, and sunflower seeds are all high in polyunsaturated fats.

*Hydrogenation* is a term you hear thrown around a lot. It is a process that makes vegetable oil solid at room temperature. Margarine is often held up as the quintessential example of a hydrogenated fat. All beneficial essential fatty acids are destroyed in the process, and much-maligned trans fatty acids are created.

## General Guidelines

For baked goods, I like to use good old-fashioned natural, fresh organic butter. For roasting or baking at higher temperatures, I usually toss foods with a couple tablespoons of heated clarified butter instead of the more volatile (relatively speaking) unrefined olive oil or the refined vegetable oils typically called for. Or if I want to use olive oil, I'll dial down the heat a bit. Good-quality olive oil is very rich in omega-9 essential fatty acids and can handle heat up to 325°F, making it quite versatile for may uses. If I'm after a hint of the tropics, I use all-natural, unprocessed coconut oil, particularly in curries or cakes and cookies. For sautés, I use olive oil, clarified butter, or expeller-pressed organic sesame oil and make sure the pan never gets too hot; remember, your nose will tell you when a fat is too hot. Using high-quality, thick-bottomed pots and pans makes controlling the heat easy.

I use many of the other oils for dipping, drizzling, and livening up all sorts of recipes—in moderation though, even if they are natural, organic, unrefined expeller-pressed oils. One great way to explore the characteristic inherent to each oil is to have a tasting. Invite friends over and have each bring a different type of artisan produced oil to compare and contrast.

Many of these fats, like olive oil, coconut oil, and butter in its various forms, have played an important role in the foodways of ancient cultures. Yamuna Devi's *The Art of Indian Vegetarian Cooking* cites Vedic literature referring to ghee as "food for the brain," and coconut oil has been used for centuries in the Pacific islands, where populations had very low incidences of what we now consider Western diseases.

As far as the good fats versus bad fats debate goes, I'm much more inclined at this point to trust what Mother Nature has provided for us and stay clear of the fats and oils product developers have designed to market to us. When you are shopping for oils, ask yourself the following questions. Is this oil organic and unrefined? Does it smell and taste like the nut or vegetable it came from? And can it withstand the temperature intended?

One last sidenote to keep in mind: Many restaurants cook with the cheapest, lowest-quality partially hydrogenated vegetable oils they can get away with. I constantly see trucks pull up in front of restaurants and offload giant jugs of liquid shortening. I also see the empty jugs days later put out for the trash collectors. At this point, restaurants do not have to disclose the trans fat levels in their food, so don't be afraid to ask about what they are using as their cooking medium or salad dressing base.

## Oils and Fats to Explore

A treasure if you can find it in its purest form, ALMOND OIL has a wonderful almond taste and is perfect for accenting a wide range of recipes. If you can find high-quality, unrefined food-grade almond oil, snatch up a bottle or two and use this fragrant oil as an accent in baked goods, drizzled over grilled vegetables, or tossed with your favorite pasta.

Cultured organic BUTTER tastes unlike anything else. It melts on the back of your tongue, and its nutty milky flavor dances up into your nose, comforting all your senses. As I said before, there is nothing like it when it comes to baking. As with any dairy products you buy, make sure it comes from producers using sustainable, organic practices. Butter, yogurt, and milk should be free of artificial hormones and extraneous antibiotics, and the livestock should be raised in humane conditions. These products are better for you, better for the planet, and better for the animals.

Two other butter-based options, CLARIFIED BUTTER and GHEE, are made by removing milk solids and water from the butter over heat. The main difference between the two is that when preparing ghee, you leave the milk solids in to toast a bit before pouring off the clarified butter; this lends a distinctive rich, nutty flavor to recipes. Make up a batch using the recipe on page 199 and keep it on hand for high-temperature roasting, sautéing, and grilling.

Also known as coconut butter, COCONUT OIL is a luxurious naturally saturated fat that's solid at room temperature. The smell of pure, unrefined coconut oil is tropical, rich, and enveloping. Coconut oil got saddled with a bad rap decades ago when tests were conducted on animals using processed, hydrogenated coconut oil. If you are still nervous about using it, look into the growing amount of research and literature focusing on the health benefits of natural coconut oil. Seek out unrefined coconut oil that still has its trademark tropical smell. Coconut oil is rich in lauric acid, which facilitates brain functions and boosts the immune system. A fantastic butter substitute, coconut oil is one of the only unrefined vegetarian fats that isn't heavily compromised at higher temperatures. When substituting coconut oil for butter, use 25 percent less coconut oil, as it is more concentrated than butter, having a lower water content.

FLAXSEED OIL has an earthy, grassy, grainy flavor, and you might want to blend it with other oils to balance out its strong taste. This golden oil is one of the richest sources of important omega-3 acids—and one of the few vegetarian sources. The body requires omega-3s and other essential fatty acids for optimal health, yet the average U.S. diet is tremendously deficient in these good fats. Being polyunsaturated, it's liquid even when chilled and must be refrigerated at all times to protect it from damage. Purchase refrigerated flax oil, and be gentle with it. If you heat it or expose it to sunlight, you risk destroying its beneficial properties. Also, pay attention to expiration dates.

Richer in essential fatty acids than flax oil, HEMP SEED OIL is a beautiful golden green oil with a flavor that is subtle yet ripe and nutty. It is polyunsaturated and stays liquid when refrigerated. Hemp seed oil is great for drizzling on soups, grains, seed-rich sandwiches, and salads. Treat it as you would flaxseed oil.

If you live in a region where olives are grown, you may be lucky enough to find fresh, local extra-virgin OLIVE OIL at your local farmers' market. Look for small producers who cold-press their olives. The oil can range from golden and buttery to grassy and green. Use olive oil as soon as possible or purchase smaller bottles to start with; unlike wine, you don't want to age your olive oil. Use your best, most fragrant and flavorful extra-virgin olive oil for drizzling and seasoning recipes, not for cooking. I keep a separate bottle on hand for cooking, typically a milder extra-virgin oil, and use this for most applications that require heating the oil. Because olive oil is rich in omega-9 fatty acids, it can tolerate moderate heat applications. It is fine for sautéing over medium to medium-high heat, or you can pair it with a bit of water for a steam-sauté.

A culinary prize and priced accordingly, PISTACHIO OIL has a rich, sweet pistachio flavor and deep green color. I use it in no-heat preparations, including spreads, sauces, drizzles, and dressings.

Deep amber in color, PUMPKIN SEED OIL tastes exactly like the seeds it is pressed from. It's great drizzled over winter squash soups, whole-grain stuffings, and casseroles. Pumpkin oil is tolerant of medium-low heat, but I prefer to use it for seasoning, not cooking. It's available in both regular and toasted varieties—both delicious.

People have long valued SESAME OIL for its distinctive flavor and rich nutritional profile. This popular oil is typically available in two varieties: plain and toasted. I use plain sesame oil to cook with when clarified butter or olive oil aren't a fit. Toasted sesame oil plays a pivotal role in many Asian recipes, and it has a special place in my kitchen as well. It sends out an immediately recognizable nutty, sultry aroma and is perfect as a seasoning on anything from noodle bowls to salads.

A delicious treat, rich and fragrant WALNUT OIL is another good source of omega-3 fatty acids and is perfect for drizzling on salads, risottos, gratins, and roasted root vegetables—the list goes on and on. I tend to use walnut oil later in the year, alongside all the wonderful comfort foods that walnuts complement so beautifully. Buy it in small quantities and keep it refrigerated.

## Oils and Fats to Avoid

Also known as rapeseed oil, CANOLA OIL is produced from the seeds of a member of the mustard family and is almost always highly refined. Although it is low in saturated fat and has 10 percent omega-3 fatty acids, these fragile fatty acids become damaged in the refining process. There are better sources of omega-3s, as mentioned above, and I avoid canola altogether.

CORN OIL is also typically refined. I have seen unrefined versions of this polyunsaturated oil, but none that are organic, meaning it is almost certainly produced with genetically modified corn. I avoid it.

Touted as the perfect all-purpose culinary solution, GRAPESEED OIL is quite fashionable to cook with. It has a neutral flavor and a high smoking point (485°F), both qualities that make it a growing favorite among both chefs and home cooks. Unfortunately, most of the grapeseed oil currently on the market is refined and not organic. Because commercially grown grapes are sprayed generously with agricultural chemicals that concentrate in their seeds, which are then pressed into oil, this is one best avoided.

Besides tasting synthetic, MARGARINE is a highly processed fat. Some margarines contain up to 50 percent trans fats. There are too many great-tasting natural alternatives out there to be using margarine in your cooking.

PEANUT OIL is made by pressing steam-cooked peanuts. The resulting oil smells like delicious, warm roasted nuts. The flavor of this oil can range from quite neutral to outright peanuty. Unrefined peanut oil is readily available, but unfortunately I haven't yet seen an organic unrefined peanut oil. This is a concern, because peanuts are often rotated into heavily chemically doused cotton fields and are sprayed over and over to ward off disease. Thankfully, there's an active group of organic peanut farmers in New Mexico, and I look forward to new products from them.

# Sweeteners

The best way I can describe my vision of the future of sweeteners is to talk about salt. It wasn't until chefs began to use regionally harvested artisan salts a few years back that home cooks and the media began to appreciate the beautiful range of colors, textures, and flavors lacking in everyday table salt. Now, fleur de sel, Hawaiian sea salt, and smoked and seasoned gourmet salts are fawned over from coast to coast.

The same revolution is going to happen with granulated sugars and sweeteners. Currently, most cooks rely on highly refined white sugar as their staple sweetener, with brown sugar riding shotgun. This leaves a whole spectrum of sweeteners, particularly less-processed ones, underutilized. This oft-neglected variety of sweeteners can bring a whole new layer of depth and dimension to food and the taste experience. Some are traditionally crafted and reflect their area of origin, while others impact the body differently than the hard, fast hit you get from white sugar, and from the high-fructose corn syrup in processed foods.

I started exploring alternative sweeteners for a couple of reasons. I was on the lookout for sweeteners produced from crops that had been farmed without chemicals and pesticides. I felt that this was an important consideration because sweeteners are concentrated, and therefore pesticides and chemicals used on crops concentrate in the final product. I was also looking for sweeteners that didn't contain additives and preservatives, as well as wanting a wider range of sweeteners to call on for my cooking overall.

Sugar is so commonplace these days that most of us don't give much thought to how it is produced. Sugarcane plantations have had a devastating effect on the environment, impacting biodiversity, water supply, and soil viability. If that weren't bad enough, runoff of fertilizers and pesticides is having an unprecedented impact on aquatic ecosystems. And conditions for workers can be brutal. There are alternatives, and I'd rather spend my money supporting sustainably minded producers working in concert with the environment and giving a fair shake to their workers in fields and factories.

As far as flavor goes, the good news is that many of the alternative sweeteners are amazing. They maintain the flavor and some of the qualities of their source, whereas white granulated sugar has a sharp, hard sweetness lacking any sort of depth or dimension. Now that I don't use it anymore, I don't miss it. Instead, a whole new world of sweetness has opened up—a kaleidoscope of honeys, ribbons of caramel-hued syrups, and earthy-toned spoonfuls of fragrant sugar granules. Below, I'll describe many of the sweeteners I use regularly and what to look for when purchasing them. Chapter 5 will give more details on how to use them.

## General Guidelines

Buy a new non-white sweetener every month for a year, and at the end I suspect you will experience many of the ones I've included as favorites in the list below. The range of flavors and textures is striking. Brainstorm different ways to use them and explore different pairings as you work them into your day-to-day cooking.

## Sweeteners to Seek Out

Lighter, cleaner tasting, and less cloyingly sweet than honey, but with a similar appearance, AGAVE NECTAR is a fantastic mild-tasting sweetener that is gaining widespread popularity. It is made from the juice of the agave plant, a desert succulent also used in making tequila. It is renowned for having a low glycemic index, which is of particular importance to diabetics and anyone who has problems with blood sugar regulation. Look for 100 percent pure agave nectar. The darker amber variety retains more of the plant's natural nutrients. White Sangria with Agave Nectar and Drunken Peaches (page 169) is a good starter recipe if you aren't familiar with using agave.

BLACKSTRAP MOLASSES is a full-bodied sweetener that runs thick and black as tar. It is made from successive boilings of sugarcane, and because many of the minerals and nutrients are preserved throughout the process, it is rich in potassium and a good source of calcium, vitamin B6, and iron. Like maple syrup, molasses is sold in grades. Molasses is graded based on whether it is from the first, second, third, or fourth boiling of the sugarcane, blackstrap coming from the last. Again, because this sweetener is a concentrate, buying organic is important. It pairs beautifully with teff in the sticky spice loaves on page 189. Look for unsulfured 100 percent organic sugarcane molasses.

BROWN RICE SYRUP is a thick, slow-moving, silky slug of butterscotch-colored goodness made by cooking sprouted brown rice in water that is then evaporated. What remains is a luminescent, not-too-sweet syrup that retains some of its antioxidant properties. Look for organic or sustainably produced brands.

DATE SUGAR is made by reducing dried zahidi dates to a cooked paste, dehydrating the paste, and then breaking it into granules. I use it more as a seasoning-type sweetener, for example in the oatmeal on page 40, to shape the flavor of a dish rather than as a foundation- and volume-building sweetener, in part because it is quite expensive and temperamental (it burns at a lower temperature than white sugar).

There is a wide choice of NATURAL CANE SUGARS available; the big hurdle is figuring out which one to buy. There is no standardization when it comes to labeling, and not all naturally labeled cane sugars are of equal quality or integrity. At one end of the spectrum are products like Sucanat (pure dehydrated sugarcane juice) and Rapadura, which are the least processed. The trade-off is that they are dry, irregular, and a bit dusty in texture.

Beyond that, there are the rich, delicious "raw" cane sugars like muscovado or Barbados, Demerara, and turbinado, which, unlike commercial brown sugars, get their natural brown color from the local sugarcane juice. You then move on to a range of cane sugars that have gone through varying stages of processing until you come out the other end with a nearly white sugar—something like Florida Crystals or the organic cane sugar sold through Trader Joe's.

I generally look for natural cane sugars that are moist and similar in appearance to brown sugar, with a fine grain echoing the size of standard white sugar grains. More often than not they'll have some combination of the following words on the packaging: *natural, raw, unrefined, whole,* and/or *unbleached.*

I'm happy to report that there's a growing variety of natural cane sugars on the market now, and some are organically produced and fair trade certified (see Sources). The other day, for example, I stumbled on a beautiful and reasonably priced Muscovado and quickly snatched a pound—a find that will disappear into a batch of Mesquite Chocolate Chip Cookies on page 182 or another favorite, Sticky Teff-Kissed Spice Loaves on page 189.

One of the things I love about HONEY is that it has *terroir*: Its flavor reflects the blossoming flowers of the specific region in which it was produced. Some honeys are thick, dark, and brooding; others are light in color and bright on the tongue. Navigating your way through the vast landscape of honey varietals involves a lifetime of tasting. A honey appropriate for pairing with an artisan cheese might be very different than a honey for baking with, so taste different types, take notes, and try different pairings. Look for raw, unfiltered, unprocessed honey, and be aware that darker honeys contain higher levels of antioxidants. Farmers' markets are typically a great place to find honey producers who can talk you through the nuances of the different varietals.

MAPLE SUGAR, a dusty-textured, buff-colored sweetener, is made by evaporating the water out of maple syrup. It is on the pricey side, but has a lovely, deep, round maple flavor that helps you forget about the hole it leaves in your wallet. This is another sweetener I tend to use as an accent, sprinkled over yogurt, dusted on top of crepes, and sprinkled over scones, cookies, and muffins as they come out of a hot oven.

The MAPLE SYRUP market is a minefield of artificially maple-flavored syrups with little to no maple content, so be sure to read labels. Pure maple syrup is rich in important minerals like zinc and manganese and comes from boiling down the sap of maple trees. Available in various grades depending on when the sap was harvested from the tree, syrup produced from tapping early in the season yields a lighter, finer syrup, designated grade A. I actually prefer grade B, which comes from sap harvested later in the season; it's thicker and more luxurious in flavor and color. Although it's illegal, some maple producers still use formaldehyde pellets in the tap holes to extend their sap-collecting season, along with a number of other sketchy practices. Buy pure, 100 percent organic maple syrup. Store maple syrup in the refrigerator.

POMEGRANATE MOLASSES, a deep, ruby-colored syrup with a tangy-sweet flavor, is derived from the concentrated juice of the pomegranate. It is commonly used in Middle Eastern cuisine and is widely available at ethnic food markets. It is a key ingredient in one of my favorite spreads, muhammara (page 102). Look for bottles labeled "pomegranate molasses," or if you can't find that, look for pomegranate syrup made from 100 percent pomegranate juice (see Sources).

## Sweeteners to Avoid

With all of the wonderful alternative sweeteners available these days, you won't even miss white sugar or any of the other less healthful sweeteners you may have been relying on. Here are a few to avoid, and some tips on eliminating even hidden sources.

It's not just that ARTIFICIAL SWEETENERS are produced synthetically; they taste synthetic, too. And on top of that, some of the companies producing them use misleading marketing messages and have questionable safety records.

There was a time when BROWN SUGAR was a semirefined version of white sugar, and this is how its reputation for being a more healthy sweetener came about. However, with the exception of certain traditional brown-in-color sugars (like muscovado), this isn't the case anymore. Brown sugar can now be considered a "painted" sugar—white sugar that has had a bit of molasses added back in for color.

WHITE GRANULATED SUGAR, the bedrock of American baked goods, is pure sweetness stripped of any flavor and character. That's not to say it doesn't develop nice flavor compounds when heat is introduced, but there is a certain one-dimensionality to white sugar that I don't find satisfying. It comes from one of two sources: sugarcane or sugar beets, and it's white due to an intensive cooking and filtration process that renders the original plant matter into almost pure sucrose. Unless the package you are buying is labeled "pure cane sugar," it is likely you've got beet sugar.

The ironic thing about HIGH-FRUCTOSE CORN SYRUP (HFCS) is that it's one of the most prevalent sweeteners in the United States, and yet you can't find it in a standard American pantry. Nonetheless, it makes up the bulk of the sweetness in the average U.S. diet, an impressive statistic for a sweetener that didn't exist before the 1970s. HFCS consumption has exploded in the past ten years, to the point where the average American consumes almost sixty pounds of it annually in sodas, processed foods, energy bars, and a long list of convenience foods. Although it's the primary sweetener in nearly all processed foods, no one really knows what the long-term health effects of consuming this much processed fructose are. One of the best replies to the claim that HFCS is a natural ingredient came from Michael Jacobson, executive director of the Center for Science in the Public Interest: "Pretending that soda made with high-fructose corn syrup is 'all natural,' is just plain old deception. . . . High-fructose corn syrup isn't something you could cook up from a bushel of corn in your kitchen, unless you happen to be equipped with centrifuges, hydroclones, ion-exchange columns, and buckets of enzymes."

I also avoid it because it is almost certainly derived from genetically modified corn crops and processed with genetically modified enzymes; plus, it is created through a chemically intense process, and the end product bears no resemblance to the crop from which it was derived.

# Spices and Seasonings

Learning how to properly salt and season food is the single best way to elevate your cooking from something simply palatable to something special. Beyond that, I encourage you to draw inspiration from traditional global cuisines and try new herbs and spices, or new pairings of those that are familiar to you. Ethnic markets are a treasure trove of unusual vibrant-smelling herbs, colorful spices, and other flavorings.

This is such a huge topic that an entire weighty tome could be written on the subject (and many have been). This section simply outlines a few of my favorite accents. That being said, I certainly encourage you to dive in deeper by exploring the world of mixing your own curry powders and pastes, or making your own spice blends and rubs.

For the best flavor, grind spices and seasonings fresh. This goes for pepper, nutmeg, chiles, and many other spices, especially those used in baking and curries—there are few exceptions, really. Many can be ground down with a little elbow grease and a mortar and pestle, or easily with a quick whirl in a relatively inexpensive spice grinder. The difference in flavor, freshness, and fragrance is remarkable.

Seek out good sources that offer high-quality products and have a rapid turnover. Buy only an amount that you can use up fairly soon; large amounts will get stale as they sit in your cupboard for years on end.

This of course leads to one of my ongoing dilemmas: how to keep my spices organized. I've finally settled on a drawer system and found that labeling the tops of little canisters with a marker makes it easy to locate individual spices at a glance. When I arranged my spices on a shelf over a foot deep, it was hard to see what was there, and I often ended up buying the same spices over and over again.

A wonderful culinary development is the magical spectrum of SALTS available, ranging in color from slatey grays to soft shell-colored pinks and dusty blacks. Textures vary from feather-light flaky shards to sandy and fine or big and moist. I gravitate toward sea salts for their natural, softer, nonmetallic flavors and the trace minerals they contain. Look for salt from quality sources. If the sea salt you buy comes from polluted water, you're getting polluted salt. If you are just getting used to substituting sea salts for table salt, go a bit at a time, as different salts have different perceived strengths, based on the size of the salt grain and other factors. As the saying goes, you can always add but never take away.

Buy a hand-cranked pepper mill and begin to explore the variety of PEPPERS now available—a world of options beyond the standard black pepper we all grew up with. One of my favorites is the Balinese long pepper grown by Big Tree Farms in Bali. It looks like a tiny cattail and has a subtle floral fruitiness that makes it a perfect complement to Black Pepper Fig Spread, page 170. Whatever pepper you choose to buy, look for estate-grown varieties and grind only as needed, as its flavor rapidly deteriorates once ground.

Seek out dried CHILES and grind them as needed to make your own chili powder. Start by grinding up chiles of one variety and getting to know the subtleties of that particular chile before crafting your own blends. Look for dried serranos, chiles de árbol, and chipotles, which have luscious deep, smoky flavors.

# Fermented Staples

Consuming certain types of fermented foods helps maintain the friendly bacteria in the digestive tract. There are quite a few things that have a negative effect on intestinal flora in day-to-day life, including most antibiotics, alcoholic beverages, and chlorinated drinking water, so counterbalancing these influences is important. Fermentation also affects flavor, digestibility, texture, and nutrition levels in certain foods by subjecting them to a predigestion of sorts. For example, tempeh, a fermented soy product, is more easily digested than soybeans. This also explains why people with lactose intolerance can often eat yogurt.

The word *vinegar* stems from the French for "sour wine"—*vin aigre*. Unfortunately, much of the VINEGAR you encounter on supermarket shelves is a speed-aged imposter, not the real thing. Look for naturally fermented vinegars that are unpasteurized, unfiltered, and traditionally crafted. You want vinegar with a taste reminiscent of the source it came from, and anything that can be made into alcohol can conceivably be turned into vinegar. Good choices include apple cider vinegar made from fermented fresh-pressed apple juice, and wine vinegar aged traditionally.

There are many uses for MISO beyond the traditional soup you're probably familiar with. This healthful fermented soybean paste can be used as a seasoning, as a rich base for a stock, and in sauces, dressings, and marinades. Look for unpasteurized, naturally fermented miso in the refrigerator section of natural foods stares and start exploring the wide range available. The lighter, creamy-colored misos are more delicate in flavor than the darker, brown versions.

One of the building blocks of Asian cuisine, SOY SAUCE is a salty-sweet condiment that adds rich, complex depth to almost any food. The key is buying a naturally fermented soy sauce made from whole ingredients using traditional methods. Chemically processed, fast-tracked soy sauce, often produced in a single day, is a harsh-tasting distant relative to the real thing. I prefer all-natural, organic, unpasteurized SHOYU, which is available in most natural foods stores.

# chapter two

# Explore a Wide Range of Grains

# EXPLORE A WIDE RANGE OF GRAINS

Chances are you encounter a grain or two at every meal. It might be a bowl of rice alongside your curry, or maybe it's a wheat berry that has been processed into flour and baked into a loaf of bread. More often than not, these grains are a nutritional shadow of their original, straight-from-the-field, whole-grain selves—refined in one way or another and stripped of many of the natural components that make them good for us.

A whole grain is a small, self-contained, life-producing factory—a seed. If you plant one, under the right conditions it will sprout and grow. Each individual grain is made up of three main parts—bran, germ, and endosperm. Bran is the multilayered, shell-like coating of the kernel. Rich in antioxidants, B vitamins, and fiber, it protects the inside of the grain from damage by sunlight, bugs, and disease. The flavorful nutrient-packed germ is where the action happens. If fertilized, it will, quite remarkably, sprout into a new plant. It contains all the life-giving nutrients needed to produce the sprout, so it's rich in protein, fats, vitamins, and powerful phytonutrients. The endosperm is the big, starchy part of the grain between the bran and the germ, and it's what you end up with after stripping all the good stuff away through processing. It provides a fuel source when the germ sprouts, and to this end it contains primarily carbohydrates, along with some protein and small amounts of vitamins and minerals. White flour consists solely of endosperm, milled and enriched with a small handful of nutrients. When you eat refined grains, you miss out on a whole host of vitamins, minerals, and phytonutrients that aren't replaced when the bran and germ are stripped away.

Unlike refined grains, whole grains are powerful health promoters. The nutritional benefits of whole grains are huge. Even small amounts—as little as three 1-ounce servings per day—can help reduce your risk of some of the

biggest health epidemics in this country: heart disease, diabetes, stroke, a wide range of cancers, osteoporosis, hypertension, and obesity. It's generally accepted that the more whole grains you eat (to a reasonable extent), the more protection you get. It takes some time to learn to cook with whole grains, so don't try to make the transition overnight; but with time, you can increasingly substitute whole grains such as farro, oats, wheat berries, quinoa, and millet for the refined grains you're currently eating, such as white rice and pastas made from refined flours. Phasing out refined grains doesn't mean depriving yourself; a world of nutrient-packed possibilities will step up to take their place.

Historically, refined grains became prevalent for several reasons. Not only do they cook more quickly, they also don't go rancid as fast, because the nutrient-rich bran and germ, along with their fats, are stripped away. This allows for longer storage time and shelf life. So, whole grains will go bad more quickly than their refined brethren, and over time, exposure to light will chip away at their nutrients. It's best to buy grains and flours from stores with a rapid turnover, and if you have the space, store them in the refrigerator (I use Mason jars of various sizes), or at least in a cool, dark place.

It is a fantastic adventure to cook your way through the world's great heirloom grains: tiny Ethiopian teff, ancient farro, a hundred vibrant shades of whole-grain rice, and New World staples such corn, quinoa, and amaranth. In this chapter, I'll share some of my favorite grain-based recipes in the hopes of piquing your interest and encouraging you to invite more of these global culinary ambassadors into your own kitchen. Despite a recent wave of appearances on forward-thinking menus, whole grains are generally dismissed in a fog of recollections of brick-heavy whole wheat breads and "neatloafs." The shift from health-food fare to gourmet status has been a slow one. But as interest in world cuisines continues to rise, many cooks are realizing that the global spectrum of grains (and grainlike grasses and seeds) is a perfect starting point for developing creative and delicious recipes. Once you become familiar with some of these grains, draw on history, your imagination, and your own taste buds for inspiration.

# A Few of My Favorite Grains

Each batch of grains has a personality all its own, so keep in mind that there are no absolutes, only approximates when you go to cook them. Cooking times are always approximate and will vary based on how long it has been since a grain was harvested, the size of the grains, and even the characteristics of the water in your area. If you are opting to used pearled grains to cut back on cooking times (yet still benefit from a semi-whole grain), the amount of pearling will impact cooking time as well.

Here are a few of my favorite grains to cook with. This list is by no means meant to be comprehensive or encyclopedic in nature; these are just a few friends I revisit time and time again in my daily cooking.

## Fast-Cooking Grains

Cooking in under 30 minutes, all of the grains described below are easily incorporated into your repertoire. Most of these cook quickly because they're small, and their compact size also lends them impressive nutrient profiles. Because they don't have much room for endosperm, small grains contain a much higher percentage of nutrient-rich bran and germ.

Not a grain in the strictest sense, AMARANTH is actually the seeds of an herb indigenous to the Americas. The tiny seed packs a flavor punch that belies its miniature stature, and its lysine-rich, 16 percent–protein profile makes it a nutritional darling to boot. Amaranth has a texture that pops in the mouth and a pronounced green spiciness that aligns it more closely in flavor to quinoa than to some of the other true grains, like wheat and oats. Many recipes can benefit from its addition, from biscuits and pancakes to tart crusts and granola bars.

Stop thinking of MILLET as something only birds eat; it is, in fact, a staple food of almost a third of the world's population. These perfect, delicately textured butter-colored beads are as good for you as they are pretty. Easy to digest and sporting a fantastic heart-healthy magnesium content, millet is a great quick-cooking starter grain. If you have the time for the extra step, the flavor of millet generally benefits from toasting, easily done in a skillet. It brings forth a nutty flavor and tints the grains a wonderful spectrum of deep yellows and light browns. The light texture and mild flavor of millet pairs nicely with fresh alliums, such as chives, green onions, and spring garlic.

The ultimate morning grain, OATS are available in a few different forms. Whole oat berries (or groats) are equivalent in size to wheat berries, but they cook up a bit faster and are naturally sweeter, lending themselves nicely to spicy, sweet, salty, and fruity preparations. Steel-cut oats are created by cutting the groat down into smaller pieces. Old-fashioned rolled oats are produced by steaming whole groats and rolling them to varying thicknesses. Instant or quick oats are simply the thinnest or most finely cut oats. All of these variations are considered whole. Like other phytonutrient-rich whole grains, oats are famously heart-healthy. A bowl a day can reduce total cholesterol in amounts that in some cases rival cutting-edge cholesterol-lowering drugs.

Cooking QUINOA is easier than trying to figure out how to pronounce it (KEEN-wah). This small, quick-cooking grain bullied me into first purchasing it years ago with a nutritional content I couldn't ignore. High in easy-to-digest fiber and tops in protein, it has an encyclopedic vitamin and mineral profile and is positively brimming with properties thought to promote cardiovascular health, stave off certain cancers, tame headaches and migraines, provide antioxidant protection, and on and on. This is the grain credited with keeping Incan armies strong and resilient. Because the protein in quinoa is considered complete, it's an ideal grain for vegetarians concerned about getting enough protein. It includes all of the essential amino acids and is a rich source of the amino acid lysine, which promotes tissue growth and repair and supports the immune system.

While I initially purchased this grain for its nutritional perks, I kept buying it for its grassy taste and fluffed-up, creamy-while-crunchy texture. It grows in a spectrum of reds, browns, and pinks, but shades of ivory or deep red predominate in U.S. markets. Use quinoa in salads and stuffings or to add texture to quick breads and cookies. Always rinse it before using to remove the bitter saponin coating (which the plant produces to deter birds and insects). Technically not a true grain, it is related botanically to Swiss chard and beets, but it is grainlike in spirit when it comes to cooking.

One of the mightiest of the mini grains, TEFF (also spelled *tef* or *t'ef*) is the staple grain of Ethiopia. (If you're a fan of Ethiopian food, you may know teff as the ingredient used to make the spongelike bread injera; keep in mind, injera is fermented and tastes slightly tangy and quite different than how you'll experience teff in the recipes here.) Because it's rich in iron, it's credited with establishing Ethiopians as some of the best long-distance runners in the world. How can such a small grain pack such a punch? There's only room for the nutrient-rich bran and germ and not much else. I use teff in tart crusts and piecrusts, in place of cornmeal in polenta, and in a range of baked breads, cakes, and muffins. It is a very dignified-looking grain available in a deep, rich, reddish brown chestnut color or a classic ivory tone. For added depth of flavor when using teff, toast the raw grains for a few minutes in a dry pan—just until fragrant. If you can't find it locally, see Sources for mail-order suppliers.

# Slower-Cooking Grains

Don't swear off slower-cooking grains just because they aren't as convenient. With a bit of advance planning, you can cook them up ahead of time on the weekend, or in a slow cooker to utilize them on the fly throughout the week.

I often use **BARLEY** as the foundation for my risotto recipes. Whole barley takes a long time to cook, so I search out barley that has had its nutrient-rich bran coating only lightly pearled off. Pearling simply buffs off a variable amount of the outer bran coating, but not as much as a fully refined grain; let's call it semi-whole. Choose bigger grains over smaller ones that have been pearled down too far. If you have the time, hulled barley (considered whole) can be used, but this will increase your cooking time significantly and it won't be as creamy. Barley thickens up stews beautifully and absorbs surrounding flavors nicely.

Trendy, health-conscious chefs have helped make the ancient grain **FARRO** quite popular over the past few years. It was one of the first domesticated grains in Mesopotamia before other cereal grains took over as preferred grain crops. Farro has been enjoying a resurgence in interest not only because of its nutritional profile, but also because it is hearty and deeply satisfying and pairs nicely with a fantastic range of seasonal ingredients year-round. Like barley, farro can be used as an alternative grain for risotto-type dishes, and is often found slightly pearled. When shopping, look for *Triticum dicoccum*, farro's Latin name. If you can't find farro for a recipe, substitute barley and cook until tender—typically taking less time than farro.

This might strike some of you as obvious, but when you grind up a **WHEAT BERRY**, you get flour. Hard red winter wheat berries end up as higher-protein bread flours, while lower-protein soft wheat berries are ground into pastry or cake flours. Because they contain the bran and germ, all wheat berries are nutritionally intact. I typically opt for soft wheat berries at the market because they cook up into plump, chewy grains that are well suited for salads, soups, or simply seasoned on their own. Wheat berries are notorious for marathon cooking times, so if you want to save some time, soak the berries in water for a few hours or overnight prior to cooking. **CRACKED WHEAT** is simply the result of cracking the wheat berries between rollers. Cracked wheat is still nutritionally intact and much quicker to cook, but completely different in terms of how you might use it. If you've had a side dish of tabbouleh, you've had cracked wheat, and you'll be able to appreciate all of its other potential applications: as a rice substitute, as a substitute for oatmeal in the morning, or to add texture and flavor to baked goods.

You've heard it before: WILD RICE isn't actually rice; it's an annual aquatic grass, and an underutilized one at that. Its distinctive nutty flavor, hearty texture, and captivating earthy colors should make it a prime candidate for frequent use beyond holiday stuffing recipes and the occasional cranberry-flecked side dish. Its nutritional benefits are legendary: Reserves of wild rice rich in protein, iron, and B vitamins helped nourish some Native American tribes through cold, harsh winters.

A variety of wild rices are available, coming not only from their native upper Great Lakes region but from California, Washington, and Idaho as well. There are both hand-harvested and cultivated wild rices. Connoisseurs will be quick to tell you that wild rice hand-harvested from a canoe is like a fine wine, the crème de la crème, but it isn't within everyone's budget. It can be surprisingly light in color and often takes much less time to cook than its cultivated cousin, the much darker, glossy, brownish black wild rice you are likely familiar with. It's also more likely that hand-harvested wild rice hasn't been raised with harsh agrochemicals. That being said, I've had delicious cultivated wild rice too; much depends on the influence of the environment in which the rice is grown (think *terroir*), how the rice is harvested, and how it is processed. Whether you are buying hand-harvested or cultivated wild rice, price and quality varies greatly. It is certainly worth the effort to find a good source (see Sources for mail-order suppliers).

As with most grains, cooking time can vary greatly, depending on the type of wild rice you buy, when it was harvested, and how much moisture is left in each rice grain by the time you bring it home. If you want to get even more earthy, nutty flavor out of your wild rice, it just takes a bit of extra time and tenacity. After cooking the rice, drain it and toss with a bit of clarified butter. In a wide, shallow baking dish (or on a rimmed baking sheet) pop it in a preheated 375°F oven until fragrant. This brings out a whole new dimension of flavor from the grains and is worth the effort if you are showcasing the rice in a salad or for simple preparations. I don't typically make that extra effort if I'm just using the wild rice in a soup or for a textural backdrop.

# Seed-Crusted Amaranth Biscuits

2 cups whole-wheat flour

1 cup whole-wheat pastry flour

1 cup amaranth flour

2 tablespoons aluminum-free baking powder

1$^1/_2$ teaspoons fine-grain sea salt

$^1/_2$ cup unsalted butter, chilled and cut into $^1/_4$-inch dice

1$^1/_2$ cups milk, plus more as needed

1 egg white

$^1/_3$ cup mixed seeds (such as sesame, poppy, and nigella)

Butter, for serving

*If rolling and cutting biscuits isn't your thing, you can take a shortcut and make drop biscuits by adding an extra $^1/_2$ cup of milk to the dough (2 cups total). Drop the dough onto baking sheets 2 tablespoons at a time and bake as directed.*

Preheat the oven to 425°F, position a rack in the middle of the oven, and line a baking sheet with parchment paper.

Into a large bowl or food processor, stir the flours, baking powder, and salt to combine. Add the butter and use a pastry cutter or 25 pulses of the food processor to blend until the mixture resembles tiny pebbles.

If using a food processor, transfer the mixture to a large bowl. Use a fork to incorporate the 1$^1/_2$ cups milk. Keep in mind that you don't want to handle the dough too much or you'll end up with tough biscuits. The dough should be dry enough that you can roll it out with a rolling pin, yet moist enough that it doesn't crumble when you shape the biscuits. If the dough is on the dry side, work in a bit more milk, 1 or 2 tablespoons at a time.

Dust a dry countertop with flour and turn out the dough. Gather it into a mass and press it out into an oval shape $^3/_4$ inch thick. Using a 1$^1/_2$-inch biscuit or cookie cutter, stamp out as many biscuits as possible. Gather the scraps together, roll them out, and continue stamping until you are out of dough. Arrange the biscuits at least 1 inch apart on the prepared pan. Brush the tops and edges with the egg white and sprinkle generously with the seeds.

Bake the biscuits for about 12 to 15 minutes, or until the edges start to turn golden. Enjoy them split open, with a modest slathering of butter.

*Makes 18 biscuits.*

When it comes to biscuits, there are plenty of people who are never going to cross over from the White Lily flour camp. For those of you who are a bit more open-minded, I encourage you to give this recipe a shot. The selection of flours—standard whole-wheat flour paired with lighter, softer whole-wheat pastry flour and moisture-retaining amaranth flour—makes for a fresh, delicious combination and golden, flaky biscuits. The crunchy crust of toasted seeds adds an unexpected twist. Nigella seeds, also called black onion seeds, have a peppery flavor and are available in Indian and Middle Eastern markets.

# Espresso Banana Muffins

2 cups white whole-wheat flour

2 teaspoons aluminum-free
   baking powder

1/2 teaspoon fine-grain sea salt

1 1/4 cups chopped toasted
   walnuts (see page 206)

1 tablespoon fine espresso
   powder

6 tablespoons unsalted butter,
   at room temperature

3/4 cup natural cane sugar

2 large eggs

2 teaspoons vanilla extract

1 cup plain yogurt

1 1/2 cups mashed overripe
   bananas (about 3 large
   bananas)

Heat the oven to 375°F, position the racks low in the oven, and line 12 muffin cups with paper liners.

Combine the flour, baking powder, salt, 3/4 cup of the walnuts, and the espresso powder in a bowl and whisk to combine.

In a separate large bowl or a stand mixer, cream the butter until light and fluffy. Beat in the sugar and then the eggs, one at a time. Stir in the vanilla, yogurt, and mashed bananas, then briefly and gently mix in the dry ingredients; overmixing will result in tough muffins.

Spoon into the prepared muffin tin (an ice-cream scoop works well), top with the remaining 1/2 cup walnuts, and bake until golden, about 25 minutes. Fill the cups two-thirds full for regular muffins or to the brim for a big-topped version. Cool in the tin for 5 minutes, then turn out onto a wire rack to cool completely.

*Makes 12 muffins.*

This decadent espresso-flecked morning muffin with a big, walnut-crusted top is everything a muffin should be. If you need more than espresso to lure you out of bed, stir in some chocolate chunks.

# Seven-Way Steel-Cut Oats

6 cups water
$^1/_2$ teaspoon fine-grain sea salt
$1^1/_2$ cups steel-cut oats

**IF YOU'VE GOT THE TIME (OR TO PRECOOK FOR THE WEEK ON A SUNDAY NIGHT):** Boil the water in a saucepan. Add the salt and then the oats, stirring as you pour them in. Lower the heat and allow the oats to barely simmer, uncovered, for about 35 to 40 minutes. You want just a hint of activity in the pot as the oats cook down, like a sluggish lava field emitting only the occasional plop. As far as consistency goes, if you like your oats on the thin side, opt for less time. For more structure, cook a bit longer. Season with additional salt as needed.

**OVERNIGHT, READY-IN-THE-MORNING METHOD:** Boil the water in a saucepan. Add the salt and then the oats, stirring as you pour them in. Remove from the heat and cover. Leave overnight. In the morning, reheat the oatmeal you want to eat (you may need to add a bit of water to achieve the right consistency) and refrigerate the rest.

*Serves 5 at once, or a work week of tasty breakfasts for 1.*

Most people hesitate to commit to anything beyond paper-packeted instant oatmeal for breakfast, saying that anything else takes too much time. Not so. If you cook up a big batch of steel-cut oatmeal (also called Irish or Scotch oats) and store it in the refrigerator, you'll be set for the week. It reheats beautifully in just a few minutes with a bit of added water. If eating oatmeal every morning for a week sounds boring, I've provided suggestions for seven tasty accompaniments. Seasoning with salt is important; it helps the oat flavor really come forward, which is necessary even if you're going to add a sweet topping.

*Seven ways to spice up oatmeal:*

1. *This is one of my favorite versions: Drizzle the oatmeal with pomegranate molasses and sprinkle with toasted walnuts. If it is on the tart side for you, add a sprinkling of natural cane sugar.*

2. *For a tropical twist, cook the oats extra long, until they are nice and thick. Stir in 3/4 cup of unsweetened coconut milk. Top with toasted coconut, chunks of ripe mango, and natural cane sugar to sweeten.*

3. *Drizzle the oatmeal with raw honey and a handful of chopped fresh figs.*

4. *Oatmeal pairs perfectly with just about any berry. Depending on the time of year, top with a handful of spring or summer berries, a drizzle of cream, and sprinkling of natural cane sugar and enjoy outside.*

5. *Feeling decadent? Caramelize sliced bananas in a sauté pan with butter and a bit of natural cane sugar, and add to the oatmeal along with freshly grated orange zest, chopped toasted macadamias, and a capful of rum.*

6. *Oats and apples have a natural affinity. Add a scoop of extra-chunky natural applesauce, a pinch of cinnamon, and a splash of cream or milk to the oatmeal.*

7. *Top the oatmeal with chopped dates and sprinkle with date sugar to sweeten.*

Whole-wheat pastry flour keeps these pancakes light as a cloud, and wild rice flour weighs in with deep nutty and grassy undertones. If you have a hard time finding wild rice flour, you can grind the dry, uncooked grain a handful at a time in a small coffee or spice grinder until it is powder fine. You can also substitute more whole-wheat pastry flour for the wild rice flour. I highly recommend that you add the optional cooked wild rice; it provides another layer of flavor as well as a nice textural twist. These pancakes are so rich and flavorful that they don't require much garnish at all beyond a melty pat of butter. I serve them with mesquite syrup or summer berry coulis on the side for light dipping; good-quality maple syrup is delicious as well.

# Wild Rice Flour Pancakes

2 tablespoons unsalted butter

1¹/₂ cups whole-wheat pastry
   flour

¹/₂ cup wild rice flour

1 teaspoon aluminum-free
   baking powder

¹/₂ teaspoon baking soda

¹/₃ cup natural cane sugar

¹/₂ teaspoon fine-grain sea salt

2¹/₄ cups buttermilk

2 large eggs, lightly beaten

1 cup cooked wild rice (optional)

Butter, for serving

Summer Berry Coulis (page 191)
   or Mesquite Syrup (page 202),
   for serving

Melt the butter in the skillet or griddle you'll use to cook the pancakes. Combine the flours, baking powder, baking soda, sugar, and salt in a large bowl, then add the buttermilk, eggs, and the reserved melted butter. Stir until all of the ingredients are just combined. Don't worry if the batter is a bit lumpy; if you overmix, you're more likely to end up with tough pancakes.

Heat the skillet or griddle until medium-hot, brush with a bit of more butter if needed, and test the temperature. If a drop of water dances across the surface, you're in the ballpark. Sprinkle a tablespoon of the precooked wild rice in the pan and pour ¹/₃ cup of batter on top of the rice. Cook until the bottom is deep golden in color, about 3 minutes, then flip with a spatula and cook the other side until golden and cooked through. Repeat with the remaining batter.

Serve with a golden pat of butter and the summer berry coulis or mesquite syrup on the side.

*Makes about 12 large pancakes.*

*Feel free to make the batter the night before; just store it in the fridge, tightly covered, until the skillet's ready. (And no need to bring the batter to room temperature; the first cakes may just take an extra minute or two to cook.)*

# Grain-ola

4 cups old-fashioned or quick-cooking rolled oats

3/4 cup unsalted raw sunflower seeds

1 cup walnuts or macadamia nuts, chopped into halves or quarters

1 1/2 cups unsweetened shredded coconut

1 1/2 cups assorted unsulfured dried fruits (try tropical fruits like dried pineapple and dried papaya), chopped

Grated zest of 2 oranges

3/4 cup raw mild-flavored honey

1/4 cup coconut oil

Preheat the oven to 300°F and set aside 2 rimmed baking sheets.

Combine the oats, sunflower seeds, walnuts, coconut, dried fruits, and zest in a large bowl. Heat the honey and coconut oil in a small saucepan over low heat, whisk to thoroughly combine, then pour over the oat mixture and stir until everything is well coated.

Divide the mixture between the baking sheets and spread into a thin layer. Bake, stirring every 10 minutes, for about 40 minutes, until toasty golden brown. Cool completely, then store in an airtight container at room temperature.

*Makes about 10 cups.*

Although we think of granola as health food, many of the versions currently available are made with highly processed oils and refined sweeteners. This granola, a favorite of mine, is a mix of honey- and citrus-kissed oats toasted until golden and then tossed with a colorful selection of dried tropical fruits. It keeps well stored in a glass jar and makes a great housewarming gift. Serve with creamy, cultured yogurt and fresh fruit for a perfect pairing.

This is the perfect pocket snack: packed with crisp brown rice, toasted walnuts, and hearty oats and accented with the tangy, sweet flavor of dried cranberries and the zing of crystallized ginger. Wrap individually in waxed paper for a great snack on the go. Be sure to look for cereal labeled *crisp* rather than *puffed*.

# Do-It-Yourself Power Bars

1 tablespoon coconut oil

1¹/₄ cups rolled oats

1¹/₄ cups chopped toasted
   walnuts (see page 206)

¹/₂ cup oat bran

1¹/₂ cups unsweetened crisp
   brown rice cereal

1 cup dried cranberries, coarsely
   chopped

3 tablespoons finely chopped
   crystallized ginger

1 cup brown rice syrup

¹/₄ cup natural cane sugar

1 teaspoon pure vanilla extract

¹/₂ teaspoon fine-grain sea salt

Grease a baking pan with the coconut oil. If you like thick power bars, opt for an 8 by 8-inch pan; for thinner bars, use a 9 by 13-inch pan.

Mix the oats, walnuts, oat bran, cereal, cranberries, and ginger together in a large bowl and set aside. Combine the rice syrup, sugar, vanilla, and salt in a small saucepan over medium heat and stir constantly as it comes to a boil and thickens just a bit, about 4 minutes. Pour over the oat mixture and stir until the syrup is evenly incorporated.

Spread into the prepared pan and cool to room temperature before cutting into whatever size bars you desire.

*Makes 16 to 24 bars.*

# Quinoa and Corn Flour Crepes
*with Chile de Árbol Sauce*

**CREPE BATTER**

2 cups quinoa flour

1 cup whole–grain corn flour (not cornmeal)

1$^1$/$_2$ cups white whole–wheat flour

$^1$/$_2$ teaspoon fine–grain sea salt

6 large eggs, beaten

2$^3$/$_4$ cups water

2 tablespoons olive oil

6 creamy potatoes (Yukon Gold or Peruvian purple), sliced so thin they are translucent

Fine–grain sea salt

Unsalted butter

2$^1$/$_2$ cups shredded Gruyère or any other flavorful melty cheese

Chile de Árbol Sauce (page 197)

1 bunch fresh chives, snipped

**TO MAKE THE CREPE BATTER**, combine the flours and salt in a bowl. Use a fork to stir in the eggs until the texture becomes raggy, then gradually stir in the water. Remove the lumps from the batter by pushing it through a strainer into another bowl. Let it rest in the refrigerator for at least 30 minutes. Stir the batter again before using. It should have the consistency of smooth heavy cream. If you need to thin with more water, do so.

To a large skillet over medium-low heat, add the olive oil and the sliced potatoes. Add a couple pinches of salt, cover, and cook until the potatoes are tender, about 10 minutes. Set aside.

**TO COOK THE CREPES**, heat a clean nonstick or well-seasoned skillet over medium heat. Rub with a touch of butter and pour just enough batter into the pan to provide a thin coating (in an 8-inch pan, this means about $^1$/$_4$ cup). As you pour, rotate the pan so the batter covers the entire bottom. Sparingly add extra batter to patch any holes, but work quickly and try to keep the crepe thin. If your batter isn't spreading easily over the pan, it is perfectly fine to thin it with more water, a couple of tablespoons at a time, and try again.

Golden-crusted pillows filled with creamy potatoes, rich, melted Gruyère, a vibrant smoky-hot sauce, and a showering of fresh-snipped chives make this my go-to crepe standard. You can make the batter a few days ahead of time and cook crepes as needed. Just about any well-seasoned or nonstick pan will work fine, but if cooking crepes becomes a regular activity, look into buying a table-top crepe maker, which will allow you to make beautiful, large, perfectly round crepes. Put the crepe maker on top of a flattened paper grocery bag for easy cleanup.

Cook until golden on one side, about 2 minutes. Flip the crepe, then top with a bit of cheese, then a few potatoes, a drizzle of chile sauce, and a sprinkling of chives. Depending on how large your crepe is, you can fold it a few different ways. If you are making crepes on the small side, either roll them or just fold them in half once or twice—the second time in the opposite direction. For larger crepes, fold two opposite sides into the middle, then do the same with the other two sides to form a square packet.

Whenever possible, make these just prior to serving. Or premake a stack of crepes, then finish off in the pan with the fillings just before serving if timing is an issue.

*Makes about 12 large crepes,*
*easily enough to serve 6 people.*

More rustic than refined, this savory soufflé is baked in buttered ramekins lined with toasted amaranth seeds. The cheesy fondue-style batter is peppered with more tiny, protein-rich amaranth grains as well as a dusting of chile powder. Try other tiny grains as well; teff would lend itself nicely to this recipe. Consider adding minced serrano chiles for extra color and zesty flavor.

# Savory Amaranth Soufflé

1¹/₄ cups whole amaranth

2 cups water

¹/₂ teaspoon plus a pinch of fine-grain sea salt

2 tablespoons unsalted butter

2 tablespoons amaranth flour

2 generous pinches pure chile powder

1²/₃ cups hot milk

6 large eggs, separated and at room temperature

³/₄ cup shredded Gruyère or any other flavorful melty cheese

Preheat the oven to 400°F and position a rack near the bottom of the oven. Generously butter four 10-ounce ramekins.

In a dry skillet over low heat, toast the whole amaranth until golden and fragrant. Sprinkle ¹/₂ cup of the toasted amaranth evenly over the prepared ramekins, coating the entire bottom and sides and shaking out any excess.

Bring the water to a boil, salt it lightly, then add the remaining ³/₄ cup toasted amaranth. Lower the heat, cover, and simmer until the amaranth is tender, about 20 minutes. Drain any remaining water, season to taste with salt, and set aside to cool.

Melt the butter in a heavy saucepan over medium heat. Add the flour, the ¹/₂ teaspoon salt, and the chile powder and cook, stirring constantly, until foamy, just 1 or 2 minutes. Do not brown. Remove from the heat and use a wire whisk to mix in the hot milk. While still whisking, return the pan to heat and bring to a boil. Keep at a boil for 1 minute; it should thicken up a bit. Remove from the heat.

Cool for just a minute or so, then use the whisk to beat in the egg yolks one at a time. Switch to a spoon and gradually add the cheese. Stir until smooth, then fold in the cooked amaranth.

Using an electric mixer, beat the egg whites with a pinch of salt until they form stiff peaks. Gently fold a big scoop of the whites into the soufflé base, then fold in the rest. Quickly (but gingerly!) fill each of the prepared ramekins to just below the rim. Put the ramekins on a baking sheet and place in the oven. Reduce the heat to 375°F and bake for about 30 minutes, or until puffy and golden. Serve immediately, if not sooner.

*Serves 4.*

# Wheat Berry Salad

*with Citrus, Toasted Pine Nuts, Feta, and Spinach*

2 cups soft wheat berries, rinsed

6 cups water

2 teaspoons fine-grain sea salt,
plus more as needed

**CITRUS DRESSING**

Grated zest and juice of 1 orange

1 tablespoon freshly squeezed
lemon juice

1 tablespoon minced shallot

1/2 cup extra-virgin olive oil

Fine-grain sea salt and freshly
ground black pepper

3 generous handfuls spinach
leaves, stemmed and well
rinsed

1 cup toasted pine nuts (see
page 206)

1/2 cup crumbled feta cheese

Combine the wheat berries, water, and 2 teaspoons salt in a large saucepan over medium-high heat. Bring to a boil, lower the heat, and simmer, covered, until plump and chewy, about an hour or so. The berries should to stay al dente, and the only way to be sure they're done is to taste a few. Drain and season to taste with more salt.

**TO MAKE THE DRESSING**, combine the orange zest and juice, lemon juice, and shallot. Whisk in the olive oil and season with a few pinches of salt and a few grinds of pepper.

Toss the hot wheat berries with the spinach, pine nuts, citrus dressing, then top with the feta. Taste for seasoning and sprinkle with a bit more salt if needed.

*Serves 4 to 6.*

Plump wheat berries shimmering with an orange-flecked citrus dressing makes this a lively winter salad, but don't hesitate to alter it to accommodate the changing seasons. For autumn, try a cranberry vinaigrette and toasted walnuts. Basil dressing with fresh heirloom tomatoes and corn would be well suited to summer. In spring, toss the wheat berries with a bit of lemon juice and olive oil, blanched asparagus segments, favas, and shelled peas. Play off the shape of the wheat berries with different serving ideas: On top of crostini or crackers, you have a twist on caviar; or wrap some up in a leaf of lettuce and you've got a new take on the spring roll.

# Toasted Wheat Germ Soup

1 cup toasted wheat germ

6 cups vegetable stock (page 203) or water

2 tablespoons extra-virgin olive oil

1 onion, chopped

1$^1$/$_2$ teaspoons red pepper flakes

1 teaspoon fine-grain sea salt

1 (14-ounce) can crushed fire-roasted tomatoes

4 cups cooked small white beans (see page 204)

Extra-virgin olive oil, for drizzling

Handful of fresh basil leaves, slivered at the last minute, for garnish

Freshly grated Parmesan cheese, for topping

Combine the wheat germ and stock in a heavy soup pot and slowly bring to a simmer over medium heat.

Meanwhile, heat the olive oil in a skillet over medium-high heat, then add the onion, red pepper flakes, and salt, and sauté until the onion starts to soften, about 5 minutes. Add the crushed tomatoes and beans and stir well, but not so vigorously that the beans fall apart. Add the tomato mixture to the simmering broth, cover, and cook over low heat for 5 minutes. Taste and adjust the seasoning.

Ladle generous portions into soup bowls, making sure to scoop deep down into the pot; the flavor tends to congregate at the bottom with the chunks of tomatoes and dense clouds of toasted wheat germ. Finish each bowl with a drizzle of olive oil, a sprinkling of slivered basil, and a dusting of Parmesan cheese.

*Serves 6.*

This Italian-inspired soup is hearty without being heavy. Rich roasted-tomato flavor and creamy beans make this a late-summer favorite. Finish with delicate slivers of fresh basil, a drizzle of your favorite olive oil, and a dusting of Parmesan. The Parmesan leaves an oozy, cheesy layer of goodness that melds perfectly with the tomato-packed broth. If you don't want to take the time to cook the beans in advance, canned beans will be fine; just drain and rinse them well.

# Quinoa and Crescenza

*with Sautéed Mushrooms*

I like to buy little pillows of Crescenza cheese and use this tangy, triple-cream cow's milk cheese to lend body, flavor, and richness to some of my favorite grain dishes. Don't panic if you can't find Crescenza; any flavorful, melty cheese will work well in this recipe. Try shredded Gruyère, Tallegio, or Brie. You can use any color quinoa you like here, and if you don't want to use alcohol, substitute a cup of water or lightly flavored vegetable stock for the white wine. Quinoa naturally has a bitter coating, so it's always important to rinse it thoroughly. One way to do this is to put the quinoa in a fine-mesh strainer and shake it under a running faucet for a minute or so.

6 tablespoons clarified butter (see page 199) or extra-virgin olive oil

1 clove garlic, minced

1/2 onion, chopped

2 cups quinoa, rinsed

1 cup good-quality dry white wine

1 teaspoon fine-grain sea salt, plus more as needed

2 cups water

2 big pinches of red pepper flakes

1 pound mushrooms, sliced 1/4 inch thick

Freshly ground black pepper

3 to 4 ounces Crescenza cheese

Heat 3 tablespoons of the butter in a large saucepan over medium high heat, then add the garlic and onion and sauté for 5 minutes, or until the onion starts to soften and get translucent. Add the quinoa, wine, and 1 teaspoon salt, bring to a boil, and continue boiling for 3 to 4 minutes, until the liquid has reduced a bit.

Add the water, return to a boil, then lower the heat, cover, and simmer for about 25 minutes, or until the quinoa opens up, revealing a little spiral, and is soft and pleasant to chew.

Meanwhile, melt the remaining 3 tablespoons butter in a large skillet over medium-high heat, along with the red pepper flakes and a few pinches of salt. Stir in the mushrooms and cook without stirring for a few minutes, until they've begun to brown and release their juices. Then shake the skillet every few minutes until the mushrooms are evenly browned, about 4 more minutes. Remove from the heat and season with salt and pepper to taste.

Once the quinoa is perfectly tender yet textured, drain off any excess liquid and stir in the cheese. Ladle into big bowls and top with the mushrooms.

*Serves 4 to 6.*

# Farro with Green Onion Sauce, Toasted Walnuts, and Asparagus

2 cups farro, picked over
and rinsed

5 cups vegetable stock
(page 203) or water

1 tablespoon extra–virgin
olive oil or clarified butter
(see page 199)

12 green onions, coarsely
chopped

$1/2$ teaspoon fine–grain sea
salt, plus more as needed

1 bunch asparagus spears
(about 1 pound), trimmed
and cut on a sharp
diagonal into 1–inch
pieces

Grated zest of 1 lemon

1 cup toasted walnuts (see
page 206), coarsely
chopped

Crème fraîche, for garnish
(optional)

Freshly grated Parmesan
cheese, for garnish

Thinly sliced green onions,
for garnish

Combine the farro and stock in a large, heavy saucepan over medium heat. Cover and simmer, stirring occasionally, until the farro is tender, 45 minutes to an hour, or about half the time if you are using semi-pearled farro.

Meanwhile, heat the olive oil in a skillet over medium-high heat, then add the chopped green onions and sauté for 5 minutes, or until the onions start to soften. Stir in a couple pinches of salt. If you have a hand blender, transfer to a small bowl and lightly puree them, but don't go overboard. Alternatively, puree them in a food processor. After a pulse or two, they will start to get nice and creamy, but you want to maintain some nice big chunks of green in there as well.

When the farro is nearly cooked, stir in the asparagus. Let the pot simmer for another couple of minutes, until the asparagus is a vibrant bright green. Some stock will still be visible in the pot. This is fine; the farro will continue to absorb the liquid once removed from the heat. Stir in the lemon zest, walnuts, and the $1/2$ teaspoon salt. Add more salt to taste if needed.

Ladle into bowls and garnish with a dollop of crème fraîche, a dusting of Parmesan cheese, and a hearty spoonful of green onions.

*Serves 4 to 6.*

Here, hearty farro grains are brightened with the clean flavors of lemon zest, green onions, and asparagus. If you are pressed for time, opt for a lightly or semi-pearled farro (the most commonly available variety), which will cut the cooking time for the grains down to about 20 minutes. Barley, both hulled and pearled, makes a nice substitution if you have a hard time finding farro.

# Grilled Polenta-Style Teff Wedges

6 cups water

1 teaspoon fine-grain sea salt, plus more as needed

2 cups brown teff grains

1 cup freshly grated Parmesan cheese

3 tablespoons melted clarified butter (see page 199) or extra-virgin olive oil

Freshly ground black pepper

Cooking these firm, polenta-style wedges on the grill brings out the sweet, toasty flavor inherent to brown teff, but feel free to use ivory teff if that is what you can find.

Line a baking sheet with parchment paper.

Bring the water to a boil in a large saucepan, then stir in the 1 teaspoon salt and the teff. Lower the heat, cover, and simmer, stirring occasionally, for about 30 minutes, or until the teff is the consistency of a thick, spreadable porridge. If it is too runny, it will spread right off the baking sheet. Stir in the Parmesan and more salt to taste.

Spread the teff polenta to a 1-inch thickness on the prepared baking sheet, then chill in the refrigerator for at least 30 minutes and preferably for a few hours. You can protect it with a layer of plastic wrap after it sets up a bit.

Prepare a medium-hot grill; if the temperature is right, you should be able to hold your hand a few inches above the grate for 4 or 5 seconds. Use a large cookie cutter or a knife to cut the chilled polenta into uniform wedges and brush each with a bit of the melted butter. Grill for a few minutes on each side, then season with salt and pepper. Serve with your choice of topping.

*Serves 4 to 6.*

*Don't have a grill? Using teff in this way lends itself to a host of different preparations:*

- **BAKED OPTION:** *Layer the wedges in a buttered baking dish and top with 1 to 2 cups of Bright Red Tomato Sauce (page 201). Bake for 30 minutes at 350°F and top with a generous amount of freshly grated Parmesan cheese and slivers of fresh basil before serving.*

- **TIME-STRAPPED ALTERNATIVE:** *Opt for a soft polenta version of this recipe whenever you don't feel like waiting for the teff to set. When the teff reaches the consistency of a creamy bowl of oatmeal, ladle it into a deep bowl and top with sautéed mushrooms, a touch of grated cheese, and a sprinkling of toasted pine nuts. If you have leftovers, they can be cooked a bit more to thicken, if need be, then slathered on a baking sheet and chilled for future grilling or cooking.*

- **GRILL-FRIENDLY TOPPING:** *Rub a couple of portobello mushrooms with olive oil, salt, and pepper and grill until cooked through. Slice thinly and serve on top of teff wedges with a sprinkling of freshly grated Parmesan cheese and snipped chives.*

- **FOR BREAKFAST:** *This polenta makes a great replacement for toast or greasy hash browns and goes wonderfully well with eggs or Curried Tofu Scramble (page 90).*

- **INDOOR VERSION:** *After barbecue season winds down, you can always finish the polenta wedges in a buttered baking sheet in a 350°F oven, or by searing them in a lightly oiled skillet.*

# Creamy Wild Rice Soup

*with Sweet Potato Croutons*

2 tablespoons coconut oil or
   clarified butter (see page 199)

1¹/₂ teaspoons red curry paste

1 large clove garlic, finely
   chopped

1 shallot, chopped

1 yellow onion, chopped

1 cup wild rice, rinsed

4 cups water

1 orange-fleshed sweet potato,
   peeled and cut into ¹/₄-inch
   dice

Fine-grain sea salt

2 teaspoons ground turmeric

1 tablespoon natural cane sugar

1 tablespoon shoyu sauce

1 (14-ounce) can coconut milk

Squeeze of lime juice

Heat 1 tablespoon of the coconut oil in a heavy soup pot over medium-high heat, then add the curry paste, garlic, shallot, and onion and sauté for 3 or 4 minutes, until the onion begins to soften. Make sure the curry paste is evenly distributed before moving on to the next step.

Stir in the wild rice and 3 cups of the water. Bring to a simmer, lower the heat a bit, and cook, covered, for about 40 minutes, or until the rice starts to soften, split, and show its fluffy insides. That being said, a surefire way to know when wild rice is tender is to taste it.

Meanwhile, prepare the sweet potato croutons. Warm the remaining 1 tablespoon coconut oil in a skillet over medium-high heat, then add the cubed potatoes and a few pinches of salt. Toss to coat the potatoes, then cook a few minutes longer, until they start to get some color on the bottom. Give them another toss to brown the other side, and continue tossing every few minutes to get more color and crispiness. If the pan dries out at all, add a bit more oil. When the sweet potatoes are cooked through and pleasantly crunchy, season to taste with salt, then scoop them out onto a paper towel.

A cold-weather soup if there ever was one—earthy, eclectic, and satisfying, with enough of a spicy kick to keep things interesting. Wild rice is cooked until plump in a rich, warm, curry-infused coconut milk broth. Each bowl of soup is topped with a crown of tiny, crisp pan-toasted sweet potato croutons.

When the wild rice is tender, stir in the turmeric, sugar, shoyu, coconut milk, the remaining 1 cup water, and 1 teaspoon salt. Stir, return to a simmer, and cook for another 5 minutes to meld the flavors. Remove from the heat and finish with a generous squeeze of lime juice. Taste for seasoning and add a bit more salt if need be. When you go to serve, ladle from the bottom of the pot to make sure each person gets plenty of rice in his or her bowl, and top with a generous sprinkling of the sweet potato croutons.

*Serves 4 to 6.*

# Otsu

**GINGER-SESAME DRESSING**

Grated zest of 1 lemon

1-inch cube fresh ginger, peeled
   and grated

1 tablespoon honey

$3/4$ teaspoon cayenne

$3/4$ teaspoon fine-grain sea salt

1 tablespoon freshly squeezed
   lemon juice

$1/4$ cup unseasoned brown rice
   vinegar

$1/3$ cup shoyu sauce

2 tablespoons extra-virgin olive oil

2 tablespoons toasted sesame oil

12 ounces dried soba noodles

12 ounces extra-firm nigari tofu

$1/4$ cup chopped fresh cilantro

3 green onions, thinly sliced

$1/2$ cucumber, peeled, cut in half
   lengthwise, seeded, and thinly
   sliced

1 small handful of cilantro,
   coarsely chopped, for garnish

$1/4$ cup toasted sesame seeds (see
   page 206), for garnish

*Unlike many pasta recipes that leave you feeling weighed down and sluggish, this one makes for a healthy, invigorating, and energizing meal that will quickly become a favorite. This recipe was inspired by a dish I enjoy often at a tiny San Francisco restaurant named Pomelo.*

**TO MAKE THE DRESSING**, combine the zest, ginger, honey, cayenne, and salt in a food processor (or use a hand blender) and process until smooth. Add the lemon juice, rice vinegar, and shoyu and pulse to combine. With the machine running, drizzle in the oils.

Cook the soba in plenty of rapidly boiling salted water just until tender, then drain and rinse under cold running water. While the pasta is cooking, drain the tofu, pat it dry, and cut into rectangles roughly the size of your thumb ($1/2$ inch thick and 1 inch long). Cook the tofu in a dry nonstick (or well seasoned) skillet over medium-high heat for a few minutes, until the pieces are browned on one side. Toss gently once or twice, then continue cooking for another minute or so, until the tofu is firm, golden, and bouncy.

In a large mixing bowl, combine the soba, the $1/4$ cup cilantro, green onions, cucumber, and about $2/3$ cup of the dressing and toss until well combined. Add the tofu and toss again gently. Serve on a platter, garnished with the cilantro sprigs and toasted sesame seeds.

*Serves 4 to 6.*

In Japanese, *otsu* means something strange, quaint, stylish, chic, spicy, witty, tasty, or romantic. In keeping with its namesake, this buckwheat noodle salad has flavor and personality to spare. Buckwheat, which technically isn't a grain, is lysine-rich and close to being a complete protein. In this recipe, buckwheat noodles (soba) are tossed with a fiery dressing tempered by a generous dose of cooling cucumbers, green onions, and pan-seared tofu. Seek out nigari tofu which is typically even firmer than other types labeled "extra-firm."

# Millet Fried "Rice"

1¹/₂ cups millet, picked over
   and rinsed
4¹/₂ cups water
2 teaspoons fine-grain sea salt
1 carrot
2 tablespoons clarified butter
   (see page 199)
2 tablespoons toasted sesame oil

2 eggs, beaten
8 ounces firm tofu, cut into
   ¹/₄-inch dice
³/₄-inch piece fresh ginger,
   peeled and grated
2 cloves garlic, minced
2 cups sliced green onions
1 tablespoon shoyu sauce

Combine the millet, water, and salt in a large saucepan. Bring to a boil, then lower the heat to an active, bubbling simmer and cook, covered, until the millet is fluffy and splitting. Test it after 20 or 25 minutes, and once it's tender but not mushy, drain off any extra water (there shouldn't be much, if any) and set aside to cool.

**TO PREPARE THE CARROTS**, use a vegetable peeler to make a pile of long shavings. Then use a chef's knife to cut into thin matchsticks. Set aside.

Heat 1 tablespoon of the butter and 1 tablespoon of the toasted sesame oil in a large skillet or wok over medium-high heat. When it is nice and hot, pour in the eggs and swirl the pan to create a thin layer of egg evenly distributed across the pan. Cook this thin omelet for about 45 seconds, or until it sets up. Fold the eggs over on themselves and cook for another 30 seconds or so before transferring the to a plate or cutting board. Let it cool a bit, then slice into strips.

You know millet. It's the tiny, round grain you most likely (and unfortunately) associate with bird seed. Lucky for us, we can enjoy it too; millet is delicious, slightly nutty, and full of important nutrients. This recipe is one of my favorite ways to use this underappreciated grain, giving an unconventional twist to traditional fried rice. You can prepare the millet a day or two ahead if you like.

Scrape or wipe any remaining egg out of the skillet, return it to medium-high heat, and, without adding any oil, drop the tofu into the pan. Cook for 4 or 5 minutes, tossing from time to time. Remove the tofu from the pan, set it aside with the sliced egg, and again, scrape out any bits from the bottom of the skillet. The pan should be clean for the next fast-moving succession of steps.

Arrange the remaining ingredients near the stove. Place the skillet over high heat, add the remaining 1 tablespoon butter and 1 tablespoon toasted sesame oil, and let the oil get hot enough that a drop of water will evaporate in a second or two when it hits the pan. Stir in the ginger and garlic and cook for about 15 seconds. Stir in the green onions and carrots, giving them a good initial toss and then stirring constantly for another 30 seconds. Stir in the millet, cooked tofu, and shoyu, cook for 30 seconds, then fold in the egg. Cook just 30 seconds longer, then taste for seasoning. I like to finish this recipe off with an extra drizzle of toasted sesame oil or a bit more shoyu.

*Serves 4.*

# Spring Minestrone

*with Brown Rice*

2 tablespoons extra–virgin olive oil

2 shallots, thinly sliced

1 clove garlic, minced

$^3/_4$ cup medium–grain brown basmati rice, rinsed

6 cups vegetable stock (page 203)

1 cup sugar snap or snow peas, trimmed and cut in half diagonally

8 spears asparagus, trimmed and diagonally sliced into 1–inch pieces

$^1/_2$ cup green peas, fresh or frozen

Fine–grain sea salt and freshly ground black pepper

Heat the olive oil in a large saucepan over medium-high heat, then add the shallots and garlic and sauté for a couple of minutes until soft. Add the rice and cook, stirring for 1 minute, then add the stock and bring to a boil. Cover, lower the heat, and simmer until the rice is just tender, 35 to 45 minutes.

Add the sugar snap peas, asparagus, and green peas, and season with a few healthy pinches of salt and a few grinds of black pepper. Simmer for another 2 or 3 minutes and serve immediately; this way the vegetables stay crisp and bright.

*Serves 4.*

When I'm in the mood for a light but nourishing soup, this is the one I turn to. The brown rice is substantial enough to make you feel full, and the asparagus and peas nicely balance the soup's flavor and texture. I build endless variations on this simple foundation. For a more Asian-inspired soup, add a couple handfuls of edamame in place of the peas and finish with a drizzle of toasted sesame oil. Or substitute shelled fava beans for the peas and finish with a bit of shaved Parmesan, lemon zest, and shredded basil for a more intensely Italian flair.

# Risotto-Style Barley

*with Winter Citrus and Arugula*

3 tablespoons extra-virgin
    olive oil

1 yellow onion, chopped

1 or 2 shallots, chopped
    (optional)

3 cloves garlic, chopped

1 teaspoon fine-grain sea salt

2 cups lightly pearled barley

1 cup good-quality dry white wine

6 cups water

1 orange

Grated zest of 1 lemon

$^1/_2$ cup freshly grated Parmesan
    cheese

$^1/_2$ cup crème fraîche or sour
    cream

2 big handfuls arugula, coarsely
    chopped

Handful of chopped toasted
    walnuts (see page 206), for
    garnish

This is a delicious,
creamy wintertime
risotto. The bright citrus
flavors pair with the bitter arugula to cut into
the creaminess of the
barley. I also like to use
watercress in place of
the arugula at times and
play around with dif-
ferent types of citrus—
grapefruit, tangerines,
tangelos—all are fair
game. If you think you'll
have leftovers, set aside
the extra portion before
adding the walnuts. It's
best to add these just
before serving.

Heat the butter in a large, heavy saucepan over medium heat, then add the onion, shallots, garlic, and salt and sauté, stirring constantly, for about 4 minutes, or until the onion begins to soften.

Add the barley to the pot and stir until coated with a nice sheen, then add the white wine and simmer for 3 or 4 minutes, until the barley has absorbed the liquid a bit. Adjust the heat to maintain a gentle, active simmer.

In increments, add about 6 cups of water, 1 cup at a time, letting the barley absorb most of the liquid between additions; this should take around 40 minutes altogether. Stir regularly, because you don't want the grains on the bottom of the pan to scorch. You will know when the barley is cooked because it won't offer up much resistance when chewing (it will, however, be chewier than Arborio rice). I think this risotto is better on the brothy side, so don't worry if there is a bit of unabsorbed liquid in the pot.

Meanwhile, grate the zest of the orange, then peel and segment the orange. Cut the segments in half, reserving any juices that leak out. When the barley is tender, stir in the orange zest, segments and juice, lemon zest, Parmesan, and crème fraîche. Taste and adjust the seasoning if need be, then stir in the arugula. Garnish with the toasted walnuts before serving.

*Easily serves 4 to 6.*

# Yucatecan Street Corn

*with Lime, Chile Powder, and Grated Cotija*

*From my Yucatecan journal: "They serve the steamed or grilled corn in the husk. The husks are peeled back from the cooked ears to form a makeshift handle. It is then slathered in crema and sprinkled generously with grated cheese (cotija). The vendor takes one half of a lime, dips it in chile powder, and squeezes the sour, spicy juice on the corn, leaving beautiful, rustic red streaks across the cheese-flecked yellow ears."*

4 ears fresh corn, in husks
$3/4$ cup crema, for slathering
$1/2$ cup shredded cotija, for sprinkling
2 limes, halved
2 tablespoons pure chile powder
Fine-grain sea salt (optional)

Prepare a medium-hot grill; if the temperature is right, you should be able to hold your hand a few inches above the grate for 4 or 5 seconds. To prepare the corn for grilling, remove any husks other than the inner one or two layers. Peel back the inner husks but keep them attached, and discard the silk. Pull the husks back into place to protect the kernels and grill, covered, rotating a couple of times along the way, for 10 minutes. You shouldn't need to soak the corn in water if your grill is the right temperature. Peel back the husk on one ear and taste for doneness before pulling the rest off the grill. Slather each with some of the crema, sprinkle with some of the cheese, and drizzle with the juice of a half of a lime dipped in chile powder.

*Serves 4.*

One of my favorite memories from a recent visit to Mexico's Yucatan Peninsula was sitting in a spacious, tree-filled *zocalo* (the main plaza) as dusk was settling over the city of Mérida. Thousands of birds combined to form a noisy orchestra in the canopy above, and street vendors appeared one by one to set up their carts. They were preparing for the promenade of locals who would descend on the *zocalo* for an evening of eating, drinking, and dancing in the tropical heat. One of the corn vendors set up next to us, and when the crema, cheese, lime, and chile powder hit the hot corn, it gave off an aroma that ignited appetites across the spacious square.

Depending on how their carts are set up, some vendors grill the corn and others steam it, always in its husk. To re-create this, look for corn in the husk, Mexican crema (sour cream thinned with a bit of water is a reasonable substitute), and hard Mexican cotija cheese (Parmesan or pecorino can be substituted). The salt in the cheese is usually enough, but if you need more salt, mix it into the chile powder.

# Cook by Color

# COOK BY COLOR

To understand why eating from a color-rich plate is important, you have to understand phytonutrients. Simply put, if a vegetable is saturated with natural color, it's also rich in compounds called phytonutrients (*phyto* meaning "plant"), which have seemingly endless health benefits. It's no surprise that certain foods have a significant impact on our health; before the advent of modern medicine, many foods were used for their healing and preventative powers. Some cultures, and some people, still use them that way.

Some believe that the lack of phytonutrients in a diet high in processed foods is a contributing factor to many of the diseases that are epidemic in industrialized nations. While not everyone buys into that premise, there is broad consensus that phytonutrients play a wide range of roles within the body, with real and often measurable effects. Many of them promote immune and cardiovascular health and act against viruses, bacteria, and inflammation, and some play a role in cancer treatment and prevention.

One group of phytonutrients that seems to have a monumental influence on well-being, longevity, and overall heath is the carotenoids. Some, like beta-carotene (in carrots and sweet potatoes) and more recently lycopene (in tomatoes), you may have heard of. Others, like lutein, might not be on your radar quite yet, but as you'll see below, they really should be. If you can't remember their specific names, it doesn't matter; the thing to grasp is how important it is to eat a wide range of brightly colored fruits and vegetables. Eat them raw, eat them cooked, and eat them daily. It's not exactly a revolutionary concept, but as you get to know a few of these stand-out carotenoids a bit better, you'll get a sense of just how powerful they are.

This is an exciting field of nutritional science, and one that's evolving rapidly. To date, over one hundred different types phytochemicals have been identified, and research into the benefits and effects of these extraordinarily healthful compounds is exploding. I'll outline some of the more significant phytonutrients below, but for obvious reasons, this list is by no means complete.

LYCOPENE (LY-co-PEEN) is found only in a small number of red-fleshed fruits and vegetables; luckily, they are all readily available and familiar: tomatoes, watermelon, and red peppers. Among other things, lycopene appears to be a particularly vigilant protector against cancer, specifically cancers of areas nobody wants to have problems with: the prostate, testes, adrenal glands, and cervix.

There is a lot of concern surrounding men and prostate health, and for good reason. In 2003, nearly 221,000 new cases of prostate cancer were diagnosed. The good news is that lycopene-rich foods seem to be not only powerfully preventative, but also therapeutic when it comes to prostate health. Lycopene appears to be good for other part of the body as well. Women who regularly consume it have five times less risk of developing precancerous conditions of the cervix, and men with the lowest levels of lycopene in their system were twice as likely to suffer a heart attack compared to those with the highest levels. Similarly impressive results have been seen in women. It's good for the skin and can naturally increase the skin's ability to protect itself from damaging radiation, essentially functioning as an internal sun block and giving you greater protection on a day-to-day basis. To get the most benefit from lycopene-rich foods, eat them with a bit of fat or oil. The fat helps make the nutrients bioavailable (more readily absorbed or useful to the body). And keep in mind that lycopene levels in the body drop off quickly, so try to replenish daily.

LUTEIN (LOO-te-an) is responsible for giving egg yolks and certain types of corn their vibrant yellow color. However, to confuse things, the richest sources of lutein are actually dark leafy greens—it's just that the lutein is covered up by chlorophyll. In the past, eye doctors have been the biggest boosters for increased lutein consumption because of its ability to dramatically impact eye health. But now that studies are beginning to show that lutein also has the ability to prevent clogged arteries, combat arthritis, and discourage colon, lung, prostate, and ovarian cancers, others are climbing on the bandwagon. One of the most impressive studies relating to lutein that I've come across demonstrated that increased lutein in the diet significantly reduces the thickening of artery walls. Powerful stuff.

BETA-CAROTENE, one of the longest-studied phytonutrients, is responsible for the yellow and orange hues of pumpkins, carrots, and sweet potatoes. The landmark research on the health benefits of beta-carotene in foods is what has fueled research into other carotenoids and phytonutrients.

One of these early studies demonstrated that getting a phytonutrient like beta-carotene from a supplement isn't the same as getting it from a whole food. In their natural state, foods high in beta-carotene were thought to reduce risk of certain cancers and prevent the accumulated damage to DNA that happens as we age. After researchers demonstrated that beta-carotene in foods did indeed help prevent lung cancer, the next logical question was whether beta-carotene supplements would do the same. This was not the case. Studies showed that smokers who took beta-carotene supplements were *more* likely to develop lung cancer. In simple terms, a nutrient isolated and dropped into the body on its own, without the benefit of working in tandem with the other nutrients present in whole foods, can have very different (and sometimes negative) effects.

Pigments found in blue and purple plants, ANTHOCYANINS fall into the flavonoid category of phytonutrients. They're highly concentrated in blueberries, blackberries, and açai. The rule of thumb is the darker the berry, the higher the anthocyanin level. Powerful antioxidants, these compounds help protect plants from a host of environmental assaults, such as UV radiation. When consumed, these compounds can protect our bodies as well. Being such strong antioxidants, they're very good at mopping up free radicals in the human body—unstable molecules triggered by environmental toxins, cigarette smoke, fried foods, burnt meat, radiation, and even by the body's own metabolic processes. Guarding against free radicals is important, as these damaging chemicals are implicated in many diseases and are thought to be a major contributor to the aging process.

Some phytonutrients can be lost or damaged during industrial processing, or even by exposure to light and heat, including during cooking. Others, like lycopene, actually become more bioavailable when combined with heat and a bit of fat. It's worthwhile to learn more about these details, but broadly speaking, if you introduce more colorful fruits and vegetables (both raw and cooked) into your diet, you are likely to reap benefits across the board.

I'm playing personal favorites in this chapter, outlining my selection of go-to foods that are rich in color and phytonutrients. This is by no means an all-inclusive list, but the foods listed below are definitely standouts, and I turn to them often in my cooking.

# Red

Deliciously beautiful lycopene-rich foods include TOMATOES, WATERMELONS, RED PEPPERS, and ROSY-FLESHED GRAPEFRUITS. Those glistening ribbons of watermelon juice running down your arms and off your elbows this summer will taste even more refreshing when you realize the good work it is doing on your insides. Looking for more ways to work lycopene-rich foods into your cooking? Spiked with extra-virgin olive oil, Bright Red Tomato Sauce (page 201) fits the bill. The pairing of tomato paste and walnuts in muhammara (page 102) is another delicious alternative, as is Roasted Tomato and Paprika Soup (page 99). Try pink grapefruit segments in a salad with nuts or avocado, or red watermelon in a yogurt-based smoothie or tossed with feta and mint for a summer salad.

While the stunning hue and tart, tangy flavor of a HIBISCUS infusion is enough to keep me coming back for more, this herb also has a deep history in healing traditions. Rich in vitamin C and antioxidants, hibiscus has been used in folk medicine to control high blood pressure, temper fevers, alleviate digestive problems, promote liver health, and improve circulatory disorders. Current studies are looking into its promising cholesterol-busting powers as well.

POMEGRANATES have been valued for their healing properties for thousands of years. Currently, Westerners are fixated on pomegranate juice for its antioxidant properties, but throughout history all parts of the tree have been used medicinally to treat everything from digestive disorders and kidney stones to fever, sore throat, and heart ailments. Roots, bark, flowers, rind, and seeds—nothing went to waste. When buying pomegranates, look for fruits that are heavy and free of blemishes, indicating pomegranates at the peak of ripeness. This is important because pomegranates don't sweeten once picked. Fruit that is starting to crack is fine as long as it doesn't look dried out. A weighty fruit means more tangy, sweet juice.

# Orange and Yellow

Also known as pot marigold, CALENDULA is one of the richest known sources of eye- and artery-friendly lutein. As far as its culinary profile goes, I've heard it called poor man's saffron. The vibrantly colored, slightly bitter petals can be integrated into your cooking in many ways: toss a few into Shredded Green Beans (page 91), sprinkle them over a summer salad, chop and add to Curried Tofu Scramble (page 90), or incorporate them into a simple compound butter by whipping minced petals into a softened stick of butter. If you can't grow your own, you can often find calendula in the herb section of your produce department as part of an edible-flower medley.

It's no news to anyone that one of the richest sources of beta-carotene (as well as being a legendary promoter of eye health) is CARROTS. Lucky for us, there are other exciting reasons to embrace them. Last year, in an animal-based study, European researchers found that a natural-occurring pesticide in carrots could reduce cancer risk by a third. Choose carrots with the deepest and most fragrant carrot scent, preferably with a lively looking bunch of greens still attached up top.

CITRUS fruits are the darlings of my kitchen. They come in a spectrum of stunning colors and range in size from the petite kumquat to the pumped-up pomelo. The range of citrus flavors goes from mouth-puckeringly tart to silly sweet. I use their zest, juice, and juicy segments every day in my cooking. And while I'm never going to come around to the idea of eating the entire orange (the pith is rich in cholesterol-reducing pectin), I'm an easy sell on the rest. Citrus appears to offer the most protection against cancers of the esophagus, mouth, larynx, and stomach. And eating just one extra serving a day can significantly reduce your risk of having a stroke. Extend your gaze beyond the navel and explore the wonderfully eclectic world of citrus. My kitchen wouldn't be the same without sweet Cara Cara and blood oranges, kumquats thinly sliced into salads, the pretty perfume of the Meyer lemon, and Buddha's hand—definitely the oddball member of the citrus family.

SWEET POTATOES play an unfortunate marshmallow-topped second fiddle to turkey on Thanksgiving tables from coast to coast and are promptly forgotten for the rest of the year. This is an unfitting fate for these delicious, albeit not so attractive root vegetables, which actually beat out carrots for the title of beta-carotene heavyweight champion—sweet potatoes, pumpkins next, and *then* carrots. So the nutritional perks you read about in regard to carrots and beta-carotene are even more true of sweet potatoes. I love their rich, sweet flavor as well as their culinary flexibility. You can bake, roast, sauté, boil, simmer, or stew them, and you can puree, mash, dice or slice them. For a truly unusual twist, sauté them into tiny croutons to top favorite soups (see page 60).

TURMERIC is a favorite of mine. I love the rich yellow-orange color and earthy, tempering flavor it brings to many curries. Steeped in history and tradition, over the centuries it has served many purposes—culinary, medicinal, and even as a textile dye. Traditional Chinese and Indian healing systems view it as a powerful anti-inflammatory, and it's been used to treat toothaches, chest pain, menstrual problems, and colic. Recent studies have been looking into its exceptional antioxidant effects, and its combination

of anti-inflammatory and antioxidant effects may help explain why people with arthritis report experiencing relief after consuming the spice regularly. Turmeric is thought to protect against a long and impressive list of ailments, including Alzheimer's, liver dysfunction, cardiovascular problems, childhood leukemia, and certain types of cancer.

# Green

One of the richest sources of folate, a B vitamin critical for healthy pregnancies, is ASPARAGUS. Without adequate folate levels before and during pregnancy, a baby's nervous system cells cannot divide properly, increasing the risk of a serious birth defect. Enjoy asparagus often when it's in season, and turn to other folate-rich foods, such as lentils, beans, and dark leafy greens, throughout the rest of the year, pregnant or not.

AVOCADOS have a decadent, creamy, potassium-rich flesh that makes them perfect for purees, spreads, dips, and soups. Consider them a nutrition booster, because eating them in conjunction with foods that contain fat-soluble phytonutrients like lutein, make those nutrients much more available to the body. To select an avocado, I put it in the palm of my hand, gently wrap my fingers around it, and squeeze very lightly. The flesh will give just a bit if it's ripe. Another way to tell is to fiddle around with the little stem button; looseness indicates ripeness.

GREEN BEANS (or string beans) have been a favorite of mine since I was a kid determined to root out (and snack on) the little green men inside. I was on to something. There is a long laundry list of benefits to reap from eating green beans: They support cardiovascular health, protect against colon cancer, and provide anti-inflammatory nutrients (good for reducing the severity of diseases like arthritis and asthma). A single cup of green beans contains 122 percent of the RDA of vitamin K, making them a strong promoter of bone health; without adequate levels of vitamin K, calcium molecules have a hard time anchoring inside the bone. And not to take away anything from spinach, but green beans have twice the iron of spinach.

SPINACH, KALE, and OTHER DARK LEAFY GREENS are some of the richest sources of vision-friendly lutein available. Some say that eye health is a mirror of overall health, and in this view it makes sense to eat your greens, especially as eye health is a big issue in the United States; over half of us suffer from cataracts by the time we are eighty. Researchers are finding that the phytonutrients in spinach also have strong anticancer properties, particularly against cancers of the colon, lung, prostate, breast, stomach, and skin. In the case of prostate cancer, active ingredients in spinach seem to cause some cancer cells to self-destruct and others to go into a state of stasis, inhibiting proliferation of the cells. Choose spinach and leafy greens that are deeply colored and vibrant, with no yellowing. Greens always seem to have dirt from the farm nestled into all those leafy crevices, so be sure to give them a good soak and rinse before using.

# Blue and Purple

Because they are so rich in anthocyanins, berries can't be omitted from a list like this. I'll give you some background on their phytonutrients here, but because I like them primarily in sweet contexts, you'll find most of the berry recipes in chapter 5. Deliciously phytonutrient-rich recipes in that chapter include Raspberry Curd Swirl Cake (page 186) and Coconut Panna Cotta with Summer Berry Coulis (page 191). Açai is paired with yogurt and featured in the chapter on superfoods (see page 127).

According to the USDA, wild berries have twice the antioxidant power of their cultivated counterparts, so if you can gather your own or purchase wild berries, by all means do so. Dried berries are another good option; they have many of the beneficial properties of their fresh cousins, but ounce for ounce they deliver a more concentrated antioxidant punch. It is important to seek out organic dried fruit, because as the fruit concentrates through drying, so do any undesirable chemical residues. A handful of dried fruit and nuts is a sophisticated alternative to croutons in just about any salad. To work more berries into your day, try tossing them into breakfast cereals (hot or cold) and making a smoothies with berries and frozen bananas.

AÇAI (pronounced ah-sigh-EE) is a Brazilian rain-forest palm berry that is starting to show up in various forms in U.S. stores: as a juice, frozen as a puree, and in products like power bars and ice creams. This superberry has a fantastic flavor—deeply rich and berry dense; some say with a hint of chocolate, but I taste a smooth vanilla finish and hint of banana in there as well. Açai contains over ten times more of the antioxidant anthocyanin than you'll find in red wine, and twice the amount in blueberries. Seek out the frozen slabs of açai puree and make your own smoothies with it.

BLUEBERRIES seem to slow and even reverse some of the degenerative diseases that besiege the aging brain, all on as little as $1/2$ to 1 cup of berries a day. It's okay to drink your blueberries; just look for all-natural unsweetened juice and spike it with sparkling water and a touch of your preferred natural sweetener.

CRANBERRIES are famous for deterring those pesky urinary tract infections. A friend affectionately calls cranberry juice "nature's broom." If you are looking for ways to use cranberries, there are many options. An easy way to start is using unsweetened cranberry juice as a drink or cocktail

### Alice Medrich's Double-Chocolate Cake

*If Sam Godfrey has looked up to anyone, it's Alice Medrich, who most recently won the IACP Book of the Year award for her cook...*

*Jackie Nickerson's 1997 portrait of a Zimbabwean farm worker, at Shainnan.*

mixer. You can boil fresh, seasonal cranberries down in a pot, cut through some of the tartness by adding a sweetener of your choice—and you will end up with a stunning topping or side dish. Strain off the berry solids, and you have a beautiful fruit syrup. Dried cranberries are also great tossed in everything from grain and green salads to stuffings. Look for unsulphured and naturally sweetened berries.

The purported powers of GOJI BERRIES bring out a certain level of fanaticism and lore. One of my favorite stories is the legend of Li Qing Yuen, a Chinese man who faithfully ate gojis and lived to the ripe old age of 252; he was fortunate enough to marry fourteen times and have eleven generations of descendants at the time of his death. In spite of the fantastic claims and hype, it's hard to ignore the significant role that goji berries (also known as wolfberries) have played in traditional Chinese medicine, being used for liver, lung, and kidney health. They're on the sweet side of tart and drier than, say, a plump, ripe raisin. I like to chop them and add to oatmeal (page 40), power bars (page 47), and granola (page 44).

PURPLE POTATOES are an example of how you can take a culinary staple (the potato), make a slightly different decision at the market (buy varietals that are rich in color), and reap nutritional benefits from that choice. While all potatoes are good sources of complex carbohydrates and potassium, colored varieties offer up a healthy dose of phytonutrients, as well as an alternative texture, different mouth feel, and a much more distinguished flavor than the starchy and all-too-common russet. Purple varieties are most commonly available, but expect a to see a range of colors, including heirloom red- and orange-fleshed varieties, in the coming years.

# Agua de Jamaica

7 cups water

1/2 cup dried hibiscus petals

1/3 cup natural cane sugar, plus
more as needed

1 lime, thinly sliced, for garnish

First off, select a pot that won't stain (pretty much anything other than a white enameled one). Hibiscus has the potential to stain just about anything it comes in contact with, including countertops, cookware, wooden spoons, and your favorite jeans.

Bring 4 cups of the water to a boil in a large saucepan and remove from the heat. Stir in the hibiscus and the 1/3 cup sugar, cover, and steep for 10 minutes, stirring once or twice along the way to help dissolve the sugar granules.

Pour the infusion through a strainer into a pitcher or jug (this is usually where something gets stained) and add the remaining 3 cups of water to the pitcher. Taste and adjust the flavor based on your personal preference, adding more sweetener or water if need be. Cool completely and serve over plenty of ice in glasses garnished with a slice of lime.

*Serves 8.*

Well chilled and served over ice, this jewel-like, ruby red infusion brims with tangy flavor from the dried petals of the hibiscus flower. Tempered with a touch of sweetener and a squeeze of crisp lime juice, this is the perfect late-afternoon refresher. Hibiscus flowers are also sometimes called jamaica flowers (pronounced ha-MIKE-uh in Spanish), and market stalls in places like the Yucatan Peninsula and Mexico City are graced with big baskets overflowing with their dried maroon petals. Here in the United States, look for dried hibiscus near the loose teas, or nestled in with bulk herbs and spices in natural foods stores. Agave nectar can step in as an alternative sweetener if you want to try something other than cane sugar. Simply sweeten to taste after straining into the pitcher.

# Curried Tofu Scramble

1 pound extra-firm tofu

1 tablespoon extra-virgin olive oil

2 cloves garlic, chopped

1 onion, chopped

2 teaspoons Sri Lankan Curry
   Powder (page 205)

3 big handfuls spinach leaves,
   stemmed

$1/2$ teaspoon fine-grain sea salt,
   plus more as needed

Drain any water from the tofu, press it between a couple of paper towels to release excess moisture, then crumble into small pieces.

Heat the oil in a heavy skillet over medium heat, add the garlic and onion, and sauté for just a few minutes, until they soften up. Stir in the curry powder and then the tofu. Cover and cook for 4 or 5 minutes, until the tofu is thoroughly heated. Add the spinach and stir for a minute or so, until it wilts and collapses, then stir in the $1/2$ teaspoon salt. Taste and adjust the seasoning. If you want a brighter curry flavor to come forward, sprinkle with more curry powder. If the flavors aren't quite popping, add more salt a couple of pinches at a time.

*Serves 4 to 6.*

I've long since given up on trying to convince certain friends that tofu scramble is a worthy culinary concept. Instead, I've resorted to a more passive approach. Slide a platter of this vibrant, turmeric-stained, spinach-rich scramble in front of any crowd of discerning palates, preferably with a side of Grilled Polenta-Style Teff Wedges (page 58) or Seed-Crusted Amaranth Biscuits (page 36), and there are few who can resist the urge to indulge. If you've got a mixed crowd on your hands, it's vegan too. Shhhh.

The firmer the tofu, the more structured your scramble is going to be. For a looser, creamier scramble, opt for a softer water-packed tofu. I love freshly ground curry powder, as called for here, but you can use just about any favorite curry powder in its place.

# Shredded Green Beans

*with Lemon-Lime Zest and Snipped Chives*

³/₄ pound green and/or yellow
    beans, tops and tails trimmed
2 tablespoons extra-virgin olive
    oil or clarified butter (see
    page 199)
2 tablespoons water

Grated zest of 1 large lemon
Grated zest of 1 lime
¹/₄ cup chopped fresh chives
Fine-grain sea salt and freshly
    ground black pepper

Slice the beans on a diagonal into roughly ¹/₈-inch pieces (look at the photograph below for guidance on how thick you should slice). If you are using a food processor, do them a handful at a time. Either way, the result should be tiny, angular zeroes.

Heat the olive oil in a large skillet over medium-high heat. Add the beans and stir until coated with oil, then add the water. Cover and cook 2 or 3 minutes, until the beans are brightly colored and tender; give the pan a good shake midway through to ensure even cooking. Remove from the heat and stir in the zests and half of the chives. Season to taste with salt and pepper and serve garnished with the remaining chives.

*Serves 4.*

Sometimes, all you need to do to breathe new life into your relationship with an overly used vegetable is to come up with a fresh way to cut it. Slice, dice, mince, chop, sliver—there are countless ways to think about size and texture in relation to food. After a lifetime of preparing whole green beans for sautés and stir-fries, seeing a traditional preparation of shredded and spiced green beans in Southeast Asia was a revelation for me. In my version, I give these nutrient-rich shredded beans a California twist by tossing in a sprinkling of chives and a combination of lemon and lime zests.

Kumquats are quirky; unlike most citrus fruits, they have a sweet peel and a tart inside, instead of vice versa. They are also a bit unusual because you can pop them in your mouth and eat them whole, reaping the nutritional benefits of consuming the whole fruit—well, almost. Eat the skins and spit out the seed or two you'll come across.

This salad is best served immediately, but if you need to make it in advance, prep all of the ingredients and keep them separate until the last minute. Once mixed and dressed, the walnuts and celery begin to get soggy. If you have a mandoline, save yourself some time and use it to shave the celery stalks.

# Clemenquat Salad

*with Walnuts and Parmesan Shavings*

6 or 7 clementines

7 stalks celery, stripped of strings

10 kumquats

3 big handfuls walnut halves,
   toasted (see page 206)

Juice of ½ lemon

2 to 3 tablespoons extra-virgin
   olive oil

Fine-grain sea salt and freshly
   ground black pepper

Block of Parmesan cheese

*This recipe calls for clementines, but tangerines, tangelos, or small oranges will also work—basically any citrus with a bit of sweetness to balance the tartness of the kumquats and the earthiness of the walnuts.*

Cut away the top and bottom ends from each clementine with a serrated knife, removing just enough to get to the flesh. Rest each clementine on one flat end and slice downward, cutting off the peel in 4 or 5 big strips. If you don't like citrus membranes, cradle the fruit in one palm and cut out each segment by running the knife between the fruit and the membrane on the sides of each segment. Otherwise, just pull the clementines into segments by hand. Either way, you'll then want to remove any seeds. Place in a bowl.

Slice the celery ⅛ inch thin on a slight diagonal (see the photograph, page 92) and add to the bowl. Using a serrated knife so as not to crush the kumquats, slice them into ⅛-inch-thick rounds and add to the bowl. When you hit seeds in the kumquats, pop them out with the tip of your knife. Add the toasted walnuts.

In a small bowl, whisk together the lemon juice, olive oil, a few pinches of salt, and a few grinds of pepper. Drizzle the dressing over the salad, then toss gently with clean hands so the fragile citrus pieces remain intact. Make Parmesan curls by running a vegetable peeler along the long side of the block of Parmesan and top each serving with a few curls.

*Serves 4 to 6.*

# Crema de Guacamole

*with Crunchy Topopos*

12 small tomatillos

3 serrano chiles, seeded and
chopped

1 white onion, chopped

4 cloves garlic, chopped

6 cups vegetable stock (page 203)

$1/4$ cup freshly squeezed lime juice,
plus more as needed

**CRUNCHY TOPOPOS**

$1/4$ cup clarified butter (see page
199), plus more as needed

12 corn tortillas, cut into thin strips

Fine-grain sea salt

$1/2$ lime

4 large ripe avocados, peeled
and pitted

$1/2$ cup loosely packed chopped
fresh cilantro

$1/2$ teaspoon fine-grain sea salt

$1/2$ lime

Crema, for garnish (optional)

Fresh salsa, for garnish (optional)

1 small handful of cilantro,
chopped, for garnish

.................................................................................................................................................

Remove the husks and stems from the tomatillos. Rinse them
well, coarsely chop, and put in a soup pot along with the serranos, onion, garlic, and stock. Bring to a boil over medium-
high heat, then immediately lower the heat and simmer for 5
minutes, or until the tomatillos start losing their structure.

Puree thoroughly with a handheld immersion blender. (If
you must use a conventional blender, be careful; the hot
liquid can burst out the top and make a huge, potentially
painful mess. Try leaving the lid slightly ajar to allow steam
to escape. Cover the top with a kitchen towel and blend in
batches on low speed.) Push the puree through a strainer
and into a bowl to remove the tomatillo seeds and skins; this
is an optional step, but one I like to take because it yields an
ultrasmooth soup. Cool for 30 minutes, then stir in the lime
juice. Refrigerate until completely chilled, at least 2 hours.

Meanwhile, make the topopos. Heat the butter in a heavy
skillet until hot but not smoking. Put a small handful of the
tortilla strips into the skillet in a single layer; don't overload
the skillet or the topopos will steam rather than brown. Toss
occasionally with a metal spatula or metal tongs (my preference) until the strips are crisp and golden brown, usually 2 to
3 minutes. Transfer to a plate lined with paper towels to drain
and immediately toss the hot strips with salt and a squeeze of
lime juice. Continue in this manner until all of the strips are

This is a perfect make-ahead soup I learned about while visiting the Yucatan Peninsula. It is a stunningly beautiful, vibrantly colored refresher to savor when the sun is hot and the air is humid. Avocados lend a satisfying potassium and fiber-rich backbone, while the tomatillos and broth bring a nice light consistency. In Mexico, this soup is made with milder, more floral limes that are difficult to find in the United States. When shopping here, the second choice would be Key limes, the third choice regular market limes. This version was written using market limes, but if you find the others, use them and increase the amount of juice you use. Organic crema is hard to come by, so you may want to make your own by thinning down organic sour cream with a bit of water.

cooked. When the topopos have cooled, they can be stored in a Mason jar or plastic bag.

In a separate bowl, blend the avocados thoroughly with the cilantro, salt, and a big squeeze of lime juice, then blend into the chilled soup base. Adjust the salt and lime as needed; you should be able to taste and smell the lime, but it shouldn't be mouth-puckering. Return the soup to the refrigerator until you are ready to serve. Top each bowl with a swirl of crema, a spoonful of salsa, a sprinkling of topopos and a pinch of cilantro.

*Serves 6 generously.*

# Baked Purple Hedgehog Potatoes

*with Yogurt-Mint Dipping Sauce*

8 smallish purple potatoes

6 large cloves garlic, sliced into
  razor-thin rounds

2 tablespoons extra-virgin
  olive oil

1 teaspoon harissa

Fine-grain sea salt

**YOGURT-MINT DIPPING SAUCE**

1 cup plain yogurt

2 cloves garlic, smashed and
  chopped

1/4 cup chopped fresh mint

1/4 cup chopped fresh cilantro

1/2 teaspoon fine-grain sea salt

Freshly ground black pepper

Preheat the oven to 375°F.

Wash and dry the potatoes, or scrub them if they're dirty. Act as if you were going to cut each potato into very thin crosswise slices, but only cut 80 percent of the way through; the potatoes need to stay intact. Toss the garlic, olive oil, harissa, and a couple pinches of salt together in a small bowl. Tuck the garlic slices deep into the potato crevices and rub the outsides of the potatoes with any leftover harissa-spiked olive oil. Sprinkle the potatoes with salt and place them on a baking sheet or tuck them into a baking dish. Cover with foil and bake for 25 minutes, then uncover and bake for another 20 minutes, or until fork-tender.

While the potatoes are baking, make the dipping sauce. Combine the yogurt, garlic, mint, cilantro, salt, and a few grinds of pepper in a small bowl and stir well. Serve the potatoes with the dipping sauce on the side or drizzled on top.

*Serves 4 to 6.*

If you make a dozen or so cuts along the length of a small potato, each cut going almost but not quite all the way through, you are on your way to hedgehog potatoes. When baked, the thin slices fan out just a tad and the silhouette echoes that of a hedgehog. You can thread all sorts of goodies in between the slices to impart different flavors. This version uses thin slices of garlic coated in a spicy blend of harissa and olive oil. The yogurt dipping sauce, featuring mint and cilantro, provides a cool, refreshing counterpoint. Harissa, a fiery hot traditional Tunisian sauce, is available in Middle Eastern markets and occasionally in the ethnic foods sections of supermarkets. If you have trouble locating it, it's okay to leave it out; the potatoes will still be delicious. You may also substitute any type of new potato for the purple potatoes.

# Red Indian Carrot Soup

2 1/2 pounds carrots

3 tablespoons clarified butter
(see page 199) or extra-virgin
olive oil

3 cloves garlic, minced

2 yellow onions, chopped

6 cups vegetable stock (page 203)
or water

2 tablespoons unfiltered raw
honey (optional)

Fine-grain sea salt

3 tablespoons olive sludge or
premium extra-virgin olive oil,
for drizzling

Each year a friend of mine harvests olives from his property in Napa and cures them by slinging them over a fencepost in a pillowcase full of salt. After their tenure on the fence, they're stored in jars, where the soft, black, salty-sweet olives weep a thick olive oil sludge that collects at the bottom. Too good to waste, we put the delicious olive sludge to use in this soup made from sweet Red Indian carrots, packed with beta-carotene. If you don't have access to freshly cured olives or Red Indian carrots, top-quality olive oil and regular organic carrots will work almost as well. Look for carrots with a lively bunch of greens still attached so you'll know they're fresh.

Scrub the carrots and cut into 1-inch segments; aim for the segments to be roughly the same size so they'll all be tender at the same time. Heat the butter in a large, heavy soup pot over medium heat, then add the garlic and onions and sauté for 5 minutes, or until the onions start to get soft and translucent. Add the stock and carrots, bring to a gentle boil, then lower the heat and simmer for 30 to 40 minutes, until the carrots are just tender throughout; don't overcook. Remove from the heat and stir in the honey.

Cool for 5 or 10 minutes, then puree with a handheld immersion blender. (If you must use a conventional blender, work in batches and be careful; the hot liquid can burst out the top and make a huge, potentially painful mess. Try leaving the lid slightly ajar to allow steam to escape. Cover the top with a kitchen towel and start blending at the lowest speed.) Season the soup with a generous amount of salt and serve drizzled with the olive sludge or olive oil. For a nice autumn variation, I sometimes drizzle the soup with toasted pumpkin seed oil and top with cubes of paneer or halloumi cheese that has been sprinkled with sugar and broiled for a few minutes.

*Serves 6.*

# Roasted Tomato and Paprika Soup

5 tomatoes, cored and quartered

1 large red bell pepper, seeded and quartered

3 yellow onions, quartered

Fine-grain sea salt and freshly ground black pepper

Extra-virgin olive oil, for coating

5 cloves garlic, unpeeled

3 cups vegetable stock (page 203) or water

1/4 teaspoon smoked paprika

Preheat the oven to 375°F and position 2 racks in the middle of the oven. Rub 2 rimmed baking sheets with a thin glaze of olive oil.

Arrange the tomatoes, skin side down, on a baking sheet. Coat the bell pepper and onions with olive oil and put them on the other baking sheet along with the garlic; place the peppers skin side down as well. Give both sheets a light showering of salt and pepper, then bake until the tomatoes start to collapse and the onions start to brown and caramelize, about 45 minutes. Turn the onions if they start getting too dark on the bottom.

Peel the garlic, dump all of the roasted vegetables into a big bowl, and puree with a hand blender. Alternatively, use a conventional blender or food processor and work in batches. Blend in the stock and paprika and adjust the seasoning to taste.

*Serves 4 to 6.*

Forget the prostitutes, bong shops, and beer houses; if you've ever been to Amsterdam during one of its never-ending winters, you know the key to contentment is finding a good source for body-thawing bowls of soup. This low-maintenance soup is reminiscent of one I had at the tiny, fresh-focused Helder's Café on my last trip to the land of canals and coffee shops. Enjoy the smell of the flavors concentrating as the vegetables bask in the oven heat. A quick finishing blend delivers a smooth puree of lycopene-rich oven-roasted tomatoes and red peppers, garlic, and onions, coupled with a smoky backdrop of paprika to warm you from the inside out. A delicious use for any leftover soup is to ladle it over hot wedges of Grilled Polenta-Style Teff Wedges (page 58) or Gnocchi alla Romana (page 105).

# Muhammara-Slathered Kabobs

**MUHAMMARA**

1 tablespoon red pepper flakes,
or 1 small red chile

1/2 teaspoon ground cumin

3/4 cup toasted walnuts (see
page 206)

1/4 cup whole-grain bread
crumbs (page 206)

1/4 cup extra-virgin olive oil

2 tablespoons pomegranate
molasses

1/4 cup tomato paste

2 to 3 roasted red bell peppers
(page 203)

1/2 to 1 cup warm water

1/2 teaspoon fine-grain sea salt

2 red onions, each cut into
6 wedges

3 lemons, each cut into
4 lengthwise wedges

12 ounces extra-firm tofu, cut
into 12 equal-sized cubes

12 mushrooms

Extra-virgin olive oil, for brushing

Fine-grain sea salt

*Muhammara is a Middle Eastern spread that quickly garnered a favored position in my kitchen, and why it plays second-fiddle to hummus and baba ghanoush escapes me. Toasted walnuts round out the flavor of a beautiful red pepper base, and a rich splash of sweet pomegranate molasses lends a subtly sweet backnote to the red chile. It is the perfect medley of color, culture, and convenience. Slather it across these vibrant kabobs, and eat the leftovers with bread, crackers, pita, chips, or anything else crunchy that you have on hand.*

Prepare a medium-hot grill; if the temperature is right, you should be able to hold your hand a few inches above the grate for 4 or 5 seconds.

In the meantime, make the muhammara. Using a hand blender (preferably) or a conventional blender, puree the pepper flakes, cumin, walnuts, bread crumbs, olive oil, pomegranate molasses, tomato paste, and red peppers to a smooth, even consistency. Mix in the warm water in increments to achieve an easily spreadable consistency similar to a thick yogurt. If you're going to use it for dipping, you might want to leave it a bit thicker. Stir in the salt and adjust the seasoning if needed.

When constructing kabobs, I don't bother soaking wood skewers in water. I just load them up with food from tip to tip, which seems to solve any problems with the wood igniting. Onto 6 medium-length skewers, thread an onion wedge, a lemon wedge, a cube of tofu, and a mushroom, then repeat. Brush each kabob generously with olive oil and season with salt. Put the kabobs on the grill and cover. Cook, rotating regularly and brushing with olive oil every few minutes, until the onions are tender, about 12 minutes altogether. To eat, slather with the muhammara, slide off the skewers. and squeeze the juice from the roasted lemons over everything.

*Makes 6 kabobs.*

Look for pomegranate molasses in the ethnic foods aisle or with the sweeteners in natural foods stores. If you can't find it, substitute an equal amount of pomegranate juice. Also, selecting the right tofu is essential here. Look for the extra-firm variety swimming in minimal liquid. As a time-saver, I've used jarred roasted red peppers with good results. If you don't have a grill, the kabobs can be cooked on a baking sheet in a 350°F oven for 30 to 40 minutes.

I reserve my gnocchi-making prowess for the heavyweight of the gnocchi world—gnocchi alla romana. This is a dish that defines family-style: large, rustic, coin-shaped semolina disks are layered and baked until brown ridges of butter-infused Parmesan form a crunchy crust in all the nooks and crannies. In a break with tradition, I add generous flecks of sun-dried tomatoes for their deep flavor, concentrated nutritional profile, and rustic eye appeal.

# Gnocchi alla Romana

*with Sun-Dried Tomatoes*

5¹/₂ cups milk

³/₄ cup finely chopped dry-
packed sun-dried tomatoes

3 cups semolina flour

¹/₂ cup unsalted butter

1 cup freshly grated Parmesan
cheese, plus more for
topping

6 egg yolks

1¹/₂ teaspoons fine-grain
sea salt

3 cups Bright Red Tomato
Sauce (page 201)

*Many variations are pos-
sible. If you have sautéed
or roasted mushrooms on
hand, chop them up and
use in place of the toma-
toes, stirring them in with
the eggs. The same goes
for a couple cups of finely
chopped spinach. I've
used chopped dried figs
and a bit of sweetener for
an unusual and slightly
sweet version, and, of
course, plain is good too.*

Preheat the oven to 400°F, clear a lot of counter space, and slather a 9 by 13-inch baking dish with butter.

Combine the milk and sun-dried tomatoes in a large sauce-pan over medium heat, bring to a simmer, and simmer gently for 1 or 2 minutes, until the tomatoes have softened and rehydrated a bit. Gradually stir in the semolina flour, mixing until it begins to pull away from the side of the pan; this just takes a minute or so. Remove the pan from the heat and quickly stir in ¹/₄ cup of the butter, ³/₄ cup of the Parmesan, the egg yolks, and the salt. If you let the yolks sit on the hot dough they will cook and set up, so work them in quickly. Let cool for 5 to 10 minutes.

Put a layer of cold water on the countertop or in a large jelly roll pan—more of a glaze than a puddle. With wet hands, turn the gnocchi dough out onto the damp counter and spread into a ³/₄-inch-thick slab. I use my hands, but you could certainly use a spoon. Cut the dough into 1¹/₂-inch circles with a cookie cutter. Gather up the scraps, press them out again, and keep stamping out rounds until all the dough is used up. If the dough is too tacky to stamp, let it cool for another 10 to 20 minutes. Use a spatula to lift each gnocchi into the prepared baking dish, slightly overlapping each circle on the previous one—similar to a fanned deck of cards. Melt the remaining ¹/₄ cup butter and drizzle it over the gnocchi. Sprinkle with the remaining ¹/₄ cup Parmesan and bake, covered, for 25 minutes, then uncovered for another 20 or 25 minutes, or until golden.

About 5 minutes before the end of the baking time, warm the tomato sauce. Dust the hot gnocchi with a little more Parmesan, cut into individual portions, ladle tomato sauce over each, and serve piping hot.

*Serves 6.*

# Green-Packed Stir-Fry

*with Fresh Herbs*

Sesame oil

8 ounces extra-firm tofu, cut
   into slices 1 inch long and as
   thick as a pencil

3 cloves garlic, minced

5 green onions, chopped

1 (1-inch) piece fresh ginger,
   peeled and grated

3 small red chiles, chopped

1/2 bunch thin asparagus (about
   1/2 pound), trimmed and cut
   diagonally into 1-inch slices

1 generous handful of cashews,
   coarsely chopped

4 generous handfuls spinach
   leaves, stemmed

Grated zest and juice of 1 lime

2 tablespoons hoisin sauce

1 small handful fresh mint,
   slivered

1 small handful fresh basil,
   slivered

Fine-grain sea salt

When you have all your ingredients prepped, arrange them within arm's reach of the stove. Heat a small splash of sesame oil in a wok or large nonstick pan over medium-high heat. When the oil is hot, add the tofu and cook for a couple of minutes, until the tofu is golden. Remove from the pan. (You can also cook the tofu in a dry nonstick or well seasoned pan.)

Add another splash of oil to the wok and, as soon as it's hot, add the garlic, green onions, ginger, chiles, and asparagus. Stir for 1 or 2 minutes, then add the cashews and spinach and stir for another minute, or until the spinach wilts and collapses. Return the tofu to the pan. Stir in the lime zest and juice and the hoisin sauce. Cook for another minute, stirring constantly.

Remove from the heat and stir in the mint and basil. Season with enough salt to make the flavors pop, starting with a few generous pinches.

*Serves 2 (generously)*
*as a main dish, 4 as a side.*

When you're in the mood to hone your knife skills, this is the recipe to tackle; it's well worth every chop, slice, and sliver. Have all your ingredients at the ready before you fire up the heat. The actual stir-frying is over before you know it. This dish, one of my all-time favorites, is great when served on top of a big scoop of brown rice.

# Big Curry Noodle Pot

8 ounces dried whole-grain
    Asian-style wide noodles
    (like udon)
2 tablespoons coconut oil or
    clarified butter (see page 199)
2 cloves garlic, finely chopped
1 onion, chopped
1½ teaspoons red curry paste
12 ounces extra-firm tofu,
    cut into thumb-sized slices
    (½ inch thick and 1 inch long)

1 (14-ounce) can coconut milk
2 cups vegetable stock
    (page 203) or water
2 teaspoons ground turmeric
2 tablespoon shoyu sauce
1 tablespoon natural cane sugar
Juice of 1 lime
⅔ cup peanuts
⅓ cup slivered shallots
⅓ cup chopped fresh cilantro

Cook the noodles in plenty of boiling salted water until just tender. Drain and set aside.

You can start making the curry as the noodles cook. Heat the coconut oil in a large saucepan over medium-high heat, then stir in the garlic, onion, and curry paste and mash the paste around the bottom of the pan a bit to distribute it evenly. Cook until nice and fragrant—just a minute or two. Add the tofu and gently stir until coated with the curry paste. Stir in the coconut milk, stock, turmeric, shoyu, and sugar, bring to a simmer, and simmer gently for 5 minutes. Remove from the heat, stir in the lime juice, and add the noodles, jostling them around a bit if they're sticking together.

To serve, heap big piles of noodles into individual bowls and top with a generous ladle or two of the curry. Top with peanuts and finish each bowl with a sprinkling of shallots and cilantro.

*Serves 4 to 6.*

A slurp and slop bowl of creamy, rich, spicy, flavorful curry with a beautiful yellow coconut milk broth. Whole-grain Asian-style noodles can be difficult to find, so I've listed a supplier in the Sources section. Long, grain-free noodles made from soy are a good alternative here too.

# Straw and Hay Fettuccine Tangle

*with Spring Asparagus Puree*

**SPRING ASPARAGUS PUREE**

1 bunch asparagus spears,
   trimmed and halved crosswise

3 handfuls baby spinach leaves

2 cloves garlic

1 cup freshly grated Parmesan
   cheese, plus more for topping

1 cup toasted pine nuts
   (see page 206)

$1/4$ cup extra-virgin olive oil, plus
   more for topping

Juice of $1/2$ lemon

$1/2$ teaspoon fine-grain sea salt

4 ounces dried spinach fettuccine,
   or 6 ounces fresh

4 ounces dried egg fettuccine, or
   6 ounces fresh

---

*The folate-rich asparagus and spinach puree can be made ahead of time; store it in the refrigerator in a jar topped with a layer of olive oil. It's also great slathered on grilled vegetable panini, as a swirl in a simple potato soup, or as a sauce for pizza.*

Bring 2 pots of water to a rolling boil, one large and one medium. You'll use the large one to cook the pasta and the medium one to blanch the asparagus.

**TO MAKE THE ASPARAGUS PUREE**, salt the asparagus water and drop the spears into the pot. Cook for 2 or 3 minutes, or until the spears are bright green and barely tender. Drain and transfer to a food processor (preferably) or a blender. Add the spinach, garlic, the 1 cup Parmesan, and $3/4$ cup of the pine nuts. Puree and, with the motor running, drizzle in the $1/4$ cup olive oil until a paste forms. It should be the loose consistency of a pesto; if too thick, thin it with a bit of the pasta water. Add the lemon juice and salt, then taste and adjust the seasoning.

Salt the pasta water well and cook the pasta until just tender; you'll need less time for fresh pasta, more for dried. Drain and toss immediately with 1 cup of the asparagus puree, stirring in more afterward depending on how heavily coated you like your pasta. Serve sprinkled with the remaining $1/4$ cup toasted pine nuts, a dusting of Parmesan, and a quick drizzle of extra-virgin olive oil.

*Serves 4 to 6.*

A few years back, I decided that spinach pasta can overwhelm the more subtle flavors in a recipe, which led me to start mixing and matching pastas. Here, the egg and spinach noodles are reminiscent of the yellow of straw and the green of hay. When cooking pasta, it is important to salt the pasta water properly. How salty? Italian cooks will tell you to salt the water until it tastes like the Mediterranean Sea. The noodles will absorb the salted water and their flavor will pop in a way that isn't possible with unsalted water. Flat-tasting pasta is generally a result of undersalting the pasta water.

# Sweet Potato Spoon Bread

3 medium–large red–fleshed
  sweet potatoes

1/3 cup unsalted butter

4 large shallots, sliced into thin
  rounds

6 ounces fresh goat cheese

3/4 cup whole–wheat pastry flour
  or white whole–wheat flour

1 teaspoon onion powder

1 teaspoon salt

Freshly ground black pepper

1 cup boiling water

3 large eggs

Freshly grated Parmesan cheese,
  for garnish

In this recipe, shallot-flecked sweet potatoes are double–baked to create the perfect comfort casserole. Dollops of goat cheese punctuate the spoon bread, providing a tangy counterpart to the natural sweetness of the sweet potatoes. While it might look a bit time–intensive at first glance, this recipe is straightforward and primarily hands–off. That being said, to save time you can use leftover mashed sweet potatoes, or if you're baking sweet potatoes for another purpose, throw in a few extras for making the spoon bread later in the week.

Preheat the oven to 350°F, position a rack in the middle of the oven, and butter a 2-quart casserole dish.

Prick each sweet potato with a fork a few times, then wrap in aluminum foil. Prick the foiled potatoes, this time to allow steam to escape. Bake for 1 to 1 1/2 hours, until the sweet potatoes are fork-tender. Cool until they can be handled, then use a big, wide spoon to scoop the flesh into a bowl. Increase the oven temperature to 425°F.

Heat the butter in a skillet over medium heat, then stir in the shallots. Cook, stirring frequently, until the shallots are golden and the butter has browned, about 9 minutes.

Whisk or blend the goat cheese with a fork until fluffy and light; you may need to add 1 or 2 tablespoons of water if the cheese is on the dry side. In a large bowl, combine the flour, onion powder, salt, and a few grinds of pepper. Add a splash of the boiling water to the flour mixture and stir to make a paste. Continue adding the water a bit at a time until it is all incorporated, and don't worry if the batter is a bit lumpy. Add 3 cups of the sweet potatoes and blend with a hand blender or by hand. Stir in the sautéed shallots and all of the butter in the pan, then stir in the eggs one at a time.

Put two-thirds of the sweet potato mixture in the prepared casserole dish and top with dollops of the whipped goat cheese. Finish with dollops of the remaining sweet potato mixture. Bake for 30 to 35 minutes, until goat cheese begins to color and the potatoes have set. Serve topped with a dusting of Parmesan.

*Serves 6 generously.*

# Winter Rainbow Gratin

3 tablespoons clarified butter (see page 199) or olive oil

4 small purple and/or red potatoes, unpeeled and cut into wedges

4 small shallots

1 large red-fleshed sweet potato, peeled and cut into 1-inch chunks

4 young yellow and/or orange carrots, cut in half lengthwise if thicker than your thumb

4 green onions, trimmed

Fine-grain sea salt and freshly ground black pepper

1 apple or pear, unpeeled, cored, and cut into 6 wedges

$1/2$ cup whole-grain bread crumbs (page 206)

$2/3$ cup freshly grated Parmesan cheese

The prettiest gratin you're likely to come across, this is also a tasty alternative to the cream-soaked potato-centric classic. Crunchy bread crumbs punctuate a medley of colorful red, purple, yellow, and orange root vegetables, with chunks of apple or pear to add a layer of natural sweetness. This is satisfying comfort food packed with phytonutrients and without the cups and cups of heavy dairy.

Preheat the oven to 375°F and position a rack in the middle of the oven.

Heat the butter in your largest ovenproof skillet over medium-high heat. In a single layer, add the potatoes, shallots, sweet potato, carrots, and green onions and toss to coat. Try not to overcrowd the pan, or the vegetables will steam and not brown. If you don't have a big enough pan, split the ingredients between two skillets. Sauté over medium-high heat for about 15 minutes, shaking the pan a couple of times along the way. The vegetables should start to brown a bit and be tender but not mushy.

Remove from the heat and sprinkle with a generous dose of salt and pepper. Stir in the apple wedges. If you don't have an ovenproof skillet, transfer the ingredients to an ovenproof baking dish or casserole. Sprinkle with all the bread crumbs and half of the Parmesan cheese. You don't want to stir at this point; rather, let the crumbs and cheese perch right on top of the vegetables so they'll get nice and crunchy.

Place the uncovered skillet in the oven. Bake for about 40 minutes, tossing the vegetables with a metal spatula about halfway through. The potatoes and carrots should be golden, crispy, and caramelized where they touch the pan and soft and tender inside. When everything is caramelized and fragrant, remove from the oven and sprinkle with the remaining Parmesan. Serve straight from the skillet.

*Serves 4 to 6.*

# Know Your
# Superfoods

# KNOW YOUR SUPERFOODS

Here's a secret: You can probably make a good case for crowning many, if not most, whole foods as superfoods. Certainly a good number of the foods discussed in chapter 3 could do double duty in this chapter. However, while natural color is a great indicator of nutritional density, there's a whole host of powerful, nutrient-rich winners that, generally speaking, are quite a bit more understated in appearance.

The superfoods I'll profile in this chapter are the alliums, cruciferous vegetables, beans and lentils, nuts and seeds, sea vegetables, sprouts, tea, and yogurt. Each of these all-natural, straight-from-the-source ingredients is brimming with vitamins and minerals, wonderful flavor, and exciting potential, plus is steeped in culinary history and ripe for new interpretations. They offer nourishment, health benefits, and protection from disease. And while forward-thinking doctors and nutritionists are excited about these foods, the real challenge is, of course, getting everyone else excited about eating them. The key is in the hands of creative cooks and chefs who can explore and highlight all the different, delicious way of preparing these super-centric ingredients.

## *Alliums*

I grew up just a short drive from Gilroy, California, the garlic capital of the world. The consequence of this, of course, was a never-ending supply of garlic in our family kitchen. I suspect this early introduction sparked my appreciation for the rest of the allium family—chives, green onions, shallots, onions, and leeks—and collectively they now provide a foundational layer of flavor for a good percentage of the savory recipes I prepare. For instance, I often use a blend of chopped garlic, shallots, and onions as the base for my soups, risottos, and sautés, rather than the more traditional French mirepoix combination that so heavily features celery and carrots. In most instances, my allium base is mild enough to allow the main ingredient to be the star. I find that celery can be too dominant, and carrots too rooty for more delicate preparations. Alliums provide a clean, direct flavor that you don't get with other base ingredients.

RAW GARLIC has the strongest and most robust flavor of the alliums, and the flavor is intensified the more finely it's chopped. Cooking mellows its flavor, and roasting or toasting whole cloves until they caramelize and ooze out of their paper skins reveals a hidden sweetness. Garlic scapes are the plant's delicious but fleeting flower stalks. Look for them at farmers' markets in spring. You may occasionally find scapes from other alliums, such as leeks. They're delicious chopped and blended into fresh cheeses or in soups, such as Garlic Scape Soup (page 146).

SHALLOTS have a more refined flavor than garlic, and because of their relatively low water content, their flavor is beautifully concentrated. I use them often—sautéed or panfried and crunchy on tops of soups and salads, roasted whole, and raw in vinaigrettes and dips.

If I had to choose just one culinary herb to use, it would be a tough battle between CHIVES, basil, and thyme, but I think I would go with chives, the most diminutive of the alliums. Most chives have a mild, herbal onion flavor. Garlic chives have flatter leaves and, not surprisingly, a garlic flavor. Use either as a garnish anytime you want to impart a mild garlic or onion flavor. They're especially good in spring and summer soups, stir-fries, soufflés, panini, eggs, and crepes.

Alliums have a long history of use for promoting health. Experiment with the different alliums in both raw and cooked form to reap the full range of their benefits, which include flu prevention, lowering blood pressure and cholesterol levels, stimulating the immune system, and destroying infectious viruses and bacteria.

## Cruciferous Vegetables

Let's be honest: It can be tough to get charged up about BROCCOLI, CAULIFLOWER, BRUSSELS SPROUTS, and CABBAGE, much less TURNIPS, MUSTARD GREENS, COLLARDS, and KALE. And it's even tougher to get other people excited about them. I understand this, so in this chapter I'll share with you some of my all-time-favorite, ace-in-the-hole ways to prepare common crucifers. In addition to being delicious when cooked thoughtfully, vegetables in this family typically contain a powerful arsenal of anticancer compounds.

# Dried Beans

I love beans. Really, really love them, so bear with me if I run on. Beans, peas, lentils, and peanuts—all are part of the legume family and have pods with a row of seeds inside. Dried beans are a wonderful and inexpensive whole food, completely unrefined and unprocessed.

Each bean has a unique flavor profile, appearance, and texture. Some beans are thin-skinned and prone to rupturing when heated to anything more than a delicate simmer. Others are sturdy and stay intact, even in the proximity of a cook with a hot-tempered stove and less-than-watchful eye. Some dried beans start their journey to the table bold and showy, with colorful markings and beguiling patterns, while others are simple and nondescript. Sadly, their markings and colors often fade into faint whispers of their former vibrancy as they rehydrate and plump up in a pot of bubbling water.

Nutritionally, beans are a powerhouse of soluble fiber, iron, and protein. Seek out beans that have been harvested and dried within the past year or so (see Sources). Dried beans that have been sitting around for years take longer to cook, are more difficult to rehydrate, and are generally more difficult to work with and prepare. They may also be less nutritious. And be sure to explore heirloom varieties. Store beans in a dark cupboard where they will retain their brightness and vitality; some of their nutrients deteriorate quickly when exposed to light.

BLACK CALYPSO BEANS are known by a host of other names, including orca and yin yang, because of their distinctive, bold black and white markings. The marks fade to more of a tan and white during cooking. Mild and starchy, black calypsos are fine prepared simply, but they also provide a nice backdrop for assertive, bold flavors. Good pairings include potatoes, smoky chiles, and chopped herbs.

For serious black bean lovers, it is worth the effort to track down this shiny, jet-black heirloom beauty. BLACK VALENTINE BEANS plump up just a bit more than most turtle beans and deliver a flesh that is rich, creamy, and hearty. They are perfect for use in chilis and stews. This is the bean I use in Chocolate Turtle Bean Tostadas (page 148).

Another knockout heirloom, BUTTERSCOTCH CALYPSO BEANS have a white body punctuated by a vibrant mustard-colored eye. Thin-skinned and creamy when cooked, this bean lends itself to many delicious preparations. Pureed with pot liquor or broth, they make a wonderful, delicate-tasting chestnut-colored soup. Even better, drain them and mash into a delicious spread for crostini.

It is easy to be charmed by FLAGEOLET BEANS, petite delicacies that are often celebrated as the caviar of beans. These beautiful immature beans span a narrow range of soft colors from buff to powder green and retain their shape and color when cooked. They are far too pretty to puree. Enjoy them whole in a cassoulet or tossed in a simple vinaigrette. You don't want to overpower their fresh and subtly green, herbal flavor.

The collective groan that arises when people learn they are being served LIMA BEANS is something I'll never understand. I typically use the dried variety, and when properly cooked, they are cream-colored, buttery, and delicate, with flesh that leans toward the starchy side of the bean spectrum. To win over the lima resistant, try the Baby Lima Soup with Chipotle Broth (page 144).

Giant ivory-colored CORONA BEANS won me over the first time I tasted them in Italy. Served on a plate, they were melty and creamy in texture and drizzled with a generous thread of olive oil. Coronas look like large lima beans when dried and grow to two or three times their original size when cooked. I often use them for Giant Crusty and Creamy White Beans with Greens (page 152).

GARBANZO BEANS are quirky, pug-shaped legumes with a beloved nutty taste and buttery texture. Commonly used in hummus, falafel, salads, stews, and veggie burgers, they are culinary workhorses and very versatile. Garbanzos are also known as chickpeas and, less commonly, ceci beans. I've also come across a tiny version called the garboncito bean. It's less nutty in flavor, but fun to cook with and delicious in its own right.

Meaty, hearty, and tiny, RED NIGHTFALL BEANS look like they've been airbrushed with a quick burst of cranberry paint. They yield a deep rusty-colored pot liquor and taste much richer than a pinto. They hold their shape when cooked and provide a creamy, melty bite. Although they're hard to find, they're still a favorite.

# Lentils

As a longtime shutterbug, I find it endearing that the optical lens is named after the lentil (Latin for "lens"), whose shape it echoes. The big up side to cooking with lentils is that they are substantial, filling, highly nutritious, and relatively quick to cook. They are great cooked into stews, mashed into spreads, molded into croquettes of all sizes, and mixed into grain-based salads. Plus, unlike most dried beans, they require no presoaking. Some varieties of lentils hold their shape, while others have a tendency to turn quickly to mush. I've found that the peppery green Le Puy lentils, from

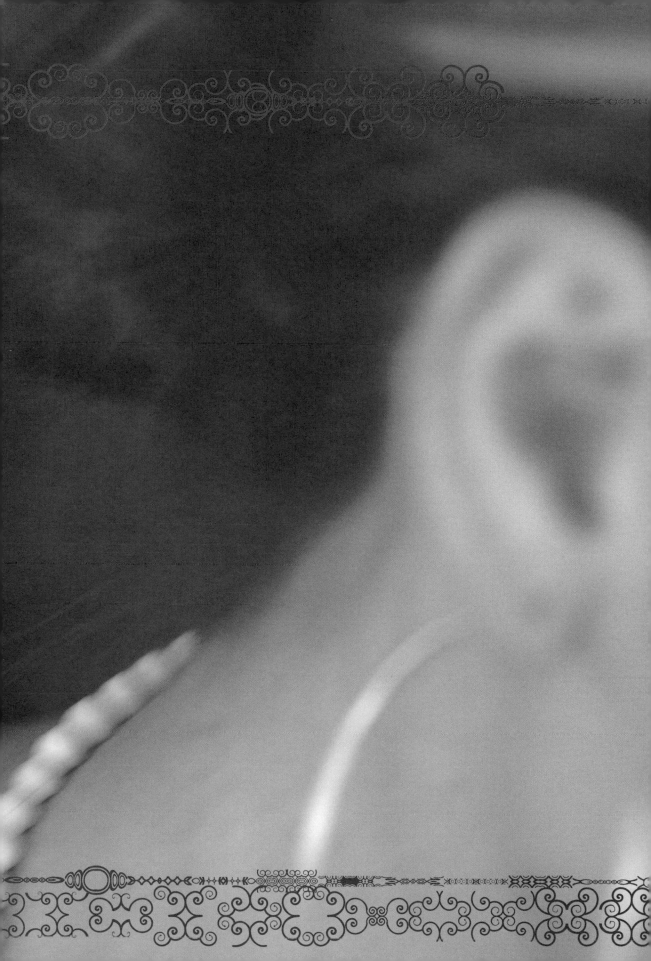

France, hold their shape nicely, as do the sexy black beluga lentils. I'm often tempted by the vibrant hues of the red and yellow varieties, but because they lose structure so quickly they are best in pureed soups or more traditional Indian preparations, such as dal. Don't let their diminutive size fool you; lentils have one of the richest protein profiles of any vegetable, backed up with super-sized levels of iron, fiber, and folate.

# Nuts and Seeds

Nuts and seeds are high in fat, but in contrast to many of the processed fats that work their way into our diets (page 16) these are natural, straight-from-the-source fats with their healthful properties intact. Start by considering a whole nut, and then imagine all the directions you can go from there. Toast that nut and the flavor becomes more pronounced. Chop it and you have a crunchy textural element to play with. Mill it into a flourlike meal and you have an ingredient that can be used to add flavor and moisture to baked goods or to deliciously thicken a pureed soup. Grind it and you have a spread or butter. Or blend it with water to make a nut milk (see Cashew Cream, page 200). Start thinking about seeds similarly. They are wonderfully diverse and span a broad range of colors, shapes, flavors, textures, and origins.

Because of their naturally high fat content, nuts and seeds can quickly go rancid. For this reason, commercial walnuts are often treated with powerful chemicals to extend shelf life. Seek out natural foods sources with a fresh stock of organic nuts, and store the nuts in the refrigerator. Nuts that are sold sliced or chopped are much more likely to be rancid upon purchase than whole nuts, and your best bet is nuts still in the shell. The shells, or even the skin as on an almond or hazelnut, adds a layer of protection from light and heat, which can cause rancidity.

ALMONDS are protein-rich and naturally a bit on the sweet side. They are amazingly versatile and work seamlessly with both sweet and savory dishes. From tarts to tagines, crostatas to claflouti, it's hard to go wrong by working almonds into your recipes.

BRAZIL NUTS are the giants of the nut world (as big as a thumb!), with a protein, calcium, and omega-3 profile to match their size. They're also up there in the fat-o-sphere alongside pecans and macadamias, with almost 70 percent fat, and a creamy flesh that lends itself nicely to pesto. You can grate them on a Microplane for a whisper-light Parmesan-like garnish.

The COCONUT is the granddaddy of seeds ( . . . or nuts . . . or fruits, depending on which botanist you consult). Wandering through a Thai market one morning, I was delighted to find a vendor making a thick, rich milk from freshly grated coconuts. The bright white liquid was captured in plastic baggies, tied off, and then sold to local cooks who inevitably packed the cream-filled balloons into baskets brimming with a rainbow of local chiles, vegetables, and herbs. Dried coconut comes in a range of thicknesses and adds a wonderful dimension of flavor and texture, especially when toasted. Also look for coconut dried and ground into a flour, a rare but delicious addition to baked goods.

FLAXSEEDS have a natural slip-and-slide quality. I avoid letting them sit around in liquid because they develop a slimy texture. Ground flaxseeds blended with water are a common substitute for egg whites in baking. A moderate sprinkling of flaxseeds on top of cereals or whole grains is a nice touch, and can help aid digestion, too.

PEANUTS are interesting because, although they are technically a legume, they store fat, rather than starches like most beans. This is what makes them so nutlike. Like other legumes, they are high in protein. It's especially important to seek out organic peanuts, because our most popular "nut" crop is, unfortunately, often rotated with cotton. Because cotton is considered a nonfood crop, it can be treated with many applications of chemicals considered too toxic for use on food. Residues of these chemicals certainly affect the following year's peanut crop. In the hot and humid South, their primary growing region, peanuts are also sprayed to keep fungus, mold, and disease at bay.

Don't make the mistake of thinking that PUMPKIN SEEDS are simply a byproduct of annual pumpkin carving. The flat green seeds, also known as pepitas, are a hallmark ingredient of Mexican cuisine and a key component in one of my all-time favorite dips, Sikil Pak (page 140), which is made from toasted pepitas pureed with pan-roasted garlic, habanero, and tomato. I prefer them toasted, and in this form they lend themselves nicely to autumn breads, soups, and salads. Ground up with spices, they provide subtle seasoning and can even serve as a base for an autumn vinaigrette.

An excellent source of omega-3 essential fatty acids, WALNUTS are commonplace in the American kitchen. Less familiar are black walnuts. If you can find black walnuts and can afford the extra cost, spring for them. The payoff is added flavor and a more rustic-looking walnut meat. Walnut-rich recipes in this book include the Clemenquat Salad (page 91) and Muhammara (page 102). They're also excellent in stuffings, salads, granola, pancakes, cookies, and quick breads.

# Sea Vegetables

A rich palette of sea vegetables awaits your discovery. They range in flavor from mild to strong and can be used to infuse a tempered saltiness and a variety of hard-to-get trace minerals into many recipes. They typically contain up to twenty times the minerals of land-grown vegetables. Sea vegetables are primarily available in dried form, which can be used as is in soups and broths. Rehydrated, they can be added to endless dishes; just soak until tender, which takes only about 5 minutes. Some types expand quite dramatically in liquid, so use a light hand until you get a feel for how much expansion to expect with each.

Toasted and crumbled, sea vegetables can be used as a seasoning, as in Toasted Nori Salt (page 205). If you aren't used to eating sea vegetables, start with milder types, such as ARAME, NORI, KOMBU, and WAKAME, and work your way up to HIJIKI, which is much stronger and actually a bit overpowering for my tastes. Wakame is the variety you often find in the bottom of your miso soup, and kombu is a natural flavor enhancer that can be used as an alternative to MSG. For a real treat, keep your eyes peeled for fresh SEA BEANS, or samphire. Though not technically sea vegetables, they grow in salt marshes and coastal estuaries and along rocky ocean shorelines, so in my book they qualify. Their quirky shape, vibrant color, and surprise saltiness make them delightful to bite into raw. They are also wonderful sautéed for just flash in a touch of good-quality olive oil.

AGAR is a sea vegetable that you're probably already eating without knowing it. An effective thickener that can be used in place of gelatin, but unlike gelatin and other thickeners, agar will set up at room temperature, making it more versatile. Give it a try in Coconut Panna Cotta (page 191).

# Sprouts

Sprouting grains, legumes, and seeds boosts their already commendable nutritional profiles. There is a lot of power and aspiration in that little sprout. Sprouts are also easier for the body to digest, so if you have had trouble with certain beans, try eating them sprouted. While growing your own sprouts is certainly an option, a wide variety of sprouts are increasingly available at farmers' markets and in produce departments. Look for bright, fresh-looking sprouts, and give them a sniff to make sure there's nothing funky going on.

# Tea

It is important to establish the difference between true tea and herbal teas right off the bat. All true teas come from a single species of plant—*Camellia sinensis.* From this modest shrub, numerous types of tea are produced: green, oolong, black, and white. Green tea is minimally processed and is generally grassy in flavor. Oolong is created from partially fermented leaves. A step beyond oolong are the black teas, made by fermenting tea leaves until they darken and develop stronger flavor. White tea comes from the same plant, but the tiny tea buds are picked before they open, when they are covered with a coat of silvery white down. Herbal teas (for example, the Agua de Jamaica on page 88) and tisanes also have healthful properties, but they are considered a separate category. Until recently, green tea has received the lion's share of accolades on the health front, primarily because it was the tea studied most extensively, but all teas are brimming with beneficial antioxidants, so enjoy exploring the spectrum. There are many ways to enjoy tea beyond just drinking it. For example, I often grind up tea leaves with a mortar and pestle and use them as a seasoning, opening up a whole new world of flavors. Rehydrated and chopped, you can use tea leaves in stir-fries, omelets, stuffings, and anything else you can dream up. Start with judicious amounts and build from there. Use too much and the tea's flavor can easily overpower other ingredients.

# Yogurt

When it comes down to something as straightforward as yogurt, the only thing that matters is finding a good source or brand. That slick packaged, synthetically sweetened stuff at the local supermarket isn't what you're after. Look for fresh organic yogurt rich in live active cultures, or if you are more ambitious, try making your own. The live cultures in yogurt help maintain an optimum balance of microorganisms in the digestive tract. This supports healthy digestion, strengthens the immune system, and provides a host of other benefits. Yogurt isn't just for breakfast or a quick snack; it has limitless culinary possibilities. If you wrap it in cheesecloth and let it drain, you'll end up with creamy, delicious yogurt cheese, to which you can add herbs, spices, or citrus zest for a savory spread, or berries and honey if you're after something sweeter. Unsweetened plain yogurt is the perfect base for many dips, such as the yogurt-mint dipping sauce on page 97 (one of my favorites). And don't miss the yogurt-based popsicles on page 127.

# Açai Power Popsicles

7 to 8 ounces frozen açai puree

3$^1$/$_2$ cups naturally sweetened
vanilla yogurt

Honey–Based Simple Syrup
(page 202; optional)

Let the açai puree soften at room temperature for 5 minutes, then crumble into a blender. Add 1 cup of the yogurt and puree until smooth. Taste, and if you like your popsicles sweeter, add honey simple syrup a tablespoon at a time.

Use the remaining 2$^1$/$_2$ cups yogurt to fill each of eight 4-ounce popsicle molds or paper cups two-thirds full. Top with the açai mixture and use the handle of a spoon to swirl the berry puree into the yogurt. Stir just enough to get some streaks going. Freeze. If you have trouble getting the popsicles out of their molds, give them a quick run under hot water.

*Makes eight 4-ounce popsicles.*

These creamy, rich, and healthy popsicles are an alternative to the artificially colored and flavored pops you see spanning the frozen food aisle. In this version, I use the freezer packs of antioxidant–rich açai puree, but any pureed frozen berries or fruit can be substituted; most pair nicely with the vanilla yogurt base. Frozen açai puree is becoming readily available in the freezer section at natural foods stores alongside other exotic fruits like the flash–frozen Amazon cherry (acerola), imported and sold under the Sambazon label. Use a high–quality, naturally sweetened, organic, full-fat yogurt for the best taste and mouth feel.

# Peach Nectar Iced Tea

4 cups cold water

4 bags black tea

4 cups peach nectar, plus more
   if desired

Plenty of ice cubes

2 peaches, peeled, pitted, and
   sliced into eighths

Mint sprigs, for garnish

Bring the water to a boil in a saucepan. Remove from the
heat, add the tea bags, cover, and steep for 5 minutes.
Remove the tea bags and, if you have the luxury of time, let
the tea cool to room temperature on the counter; this keeps it
from clouding up. Stir in the peach nectar and feel free to add
more if you want it even peachier. Serve in ice-filled glasses
garnished with a couple slices of peach and a sprig of mint.

*Serves 8.*

A well-respected chef I once spent a few days with kept
me pumped full of tall, icy glasses of wonderfully peachy
iced tea. If summertime had a flavor, this would be it. I
suspect the secret ingredient was peach nectar, and I've
been spiking my iced tea with it ever since. For a special
touch, sugar the rims of the glasses. Rub a bit of water
around each rim with your fingers and invert each glass
into a shallow bowl of fine-grain natural cane sugar.

# Beluga Lentil Crostini

*with Chèvre-Chive Spread*

1¹/₄ cups dry beluga lentils, picked over and rinsed

4 cups water or vegetable stock (page 203)

1 to 2 teaspoons fine-grain sea salt

**CROSTINI**

¹/₃ cup extra-virgin olive oil or melted butter

Fine-grain sea salt

1 whole-grain baguette or loaf, cut into ¹/₄-inch-thick slices

3 to 4 large cloves garlic

**CHÈVRE-CHIVE SPREAD**

8 ounces fresh goat cheese, at room temperature

1 small splash of milk

1 large bunch chives

Fine-grain sea salt

Snipped fresh chives, for garnish

Chive blossoms, for garnish

Preheat the oven to 350°F.

Put the lentils in a large saucepan and cover with the water. Bring to a boil, then lower the heat and simmer for 15 to 20 minutes, until the lentils are tender but not splitting or falling apart. Add the salt to the lentils at this point (use less if you've boiled them in a salty vegetable stock); adding salt now helps to prevent lentils from falling apart. Remove the pot from the heat, drain, and set aside.

While the lentils are cooking, prepare the crostini. Pour the olive oil into a large bowl and add a few pinches of salt. Add all the sliced bread to the bowl and toss well. Place the slices in a single layer across two baking sheets and bake for 10 minutes, or until slightly golden. Set aside until cool enough to handle. Cut one end off each garlic clove and lightly rub the top surface of each crostini with the garlic. Try not to overdo it; you are just after a hint of garlic.

**TO MAKE THE CHÈVRE SPREAD**, combine the goat cheese and milk in a small bowl; you only need enough milk to thin the cheese and make it spreadable. With scissors, snip the chives into the goat cheese and stir to combine. Season with a bit of salt and set aside.

Before assembling, make sure all the components are at room temperature. Top each piece of bread with a slathering of the chèvre spread and a small spoonful of lentils. Garnish with more snipped chives, and use pretty purple chive blossoms for the platter if they are in season.

*Makes about 4 dozen.*

---

Beluga lentils are very earthy tasting, with a bit of grassiness, and this plays nicely with the chives and the tanginess of the goat cheese in this recipe. You can prepare all of the components a day ahead and assemble them just before serving. A whole-grain walnut bread is a nice base. You'll have leftover lentils to experiment with; or you can use them in Chunky Lentil Soup (page 141).

# Black Tea Spring Rolls

*with Mushrooms and Mango Chutney Dipping Sauce*

1 teaspoon black tea leaves,
  preferably Lapsang Souchong
1 tablespoon sesame oil
3 shallots, chopped
1 clove garlic, minced
1 pound mushrooms, chopped
8 ounces extra-firm tofu,
  crumbled
2 handfuls spinach leaves,
  stemmed and chopped

2 tablespoons shoyu sauce
12 (6-inch) wonton wrappers
2 tablespoons melted unsalted
  butter or sesame oil

**MANGO CHUTNEY DIPPING SAUCE**
$^3/_4$ cup prepared mango chutney
$^1/_4$ cup apple cider vinegar
Pinch of ground black tea leaves

Preheat the oven to 400°F.

Grind the tea into a fine powder with a mortar and pestle or in a spice grinder. Heat the sesame oil in a large skillet over medium-high heat, add the shallots, garlic, and mushrooms, and sauté for 5 or 6 minutes, until the mushrooms release their moisture and cook down a bit. Gently stir in the tofu, spinach, and shoyu until the shoyu is evenly distributed. Taste and add more shoyu a bit at a time if need be. Season with a few big pinches of the ground tea, but reserve a generous pinch for use in the dipping sauce.

**TO ASSEMBLE THE SPRING ROLLS**, approach them as though they're a smaller version of a burrito. Place a wrapper in front of you so it looks like a diamond. Put a couple tablespoons of filling a short distance in from the corner nearest you. Take that corner and fold it over the filling, then roll it once away from you. Fold in the left and right corners, then continue rolling away from you. Dab a bit of water on the inside of that last loose corner to seal.

Arrange the spring rolls seam down on a baking sheet, brush with the melted butter, and bake for 10 minutes, turning each roll halfway through to get both sides brown and crispy.

Make the dipping sauce by whisking the chutney, vinegar, and ground tea together in a small bowl. Serve the spring rolls hot, with the dipping sauce alongside.

*Makes 12 rolls.*

Bite through a crispy wonton wrapper into this tea-seasoned, mushroom-rich filling and consider your love affair with deep-fried spring rolls in peril. In this recipe, ground tea leaves are used as a seasoning. I like to use a fragrant, smoky Lapsang Souchong to match the meaty richness of the pan-seared mushrooms. While smoky black teas are a natural fit here, I've also had delicious results with citrus peel–black tea blends, which pair nicely with the mango in the dipping sauce. Try using fresh or rehydrated yuba (thin sheets of tofu skin) in place of the wonton wrappers, if you come across it.

# Crunchy Slaw Salad

**CREAMY VINAIGRETTE**

2 tablespoons apple cider vinegar

Juice of 1 lemon

Fine-grain sea salt and freshly
ground black pepper

1/2 cup extra-virgin olive oil

Splash of heavy cream

1 extra-crisp apple, peeled and
cored

1 big squeeze of lemon juice

1 small savoy cabbage

1 cup chopped toasted walnuts
(see page 206)

**TO MAKE THE DRESSING**, whisk the apple cider and lemon juice together in a small bowl, season with a few pinches of salt and a couple grinds of pepper, then gradually whisk in the olive oil followed by the cream. Set aside.

Shred the apple on the large holes of a box grater (or use the grater attachment on a food processor), then put the shreds in a bowl of cold water with the squeeze of lemon; this will keep the apple from browning. Cut the cabbage into quarters and core each section, then cut them into a very fine chiffonade. Just before serving, drain the apples and toss with the cabbage, walnuts, and dressing in a large bowl. Taste and adjust the seasoning if needed. Serve immediately.

*Serves 4 to 6.*

The great thing about this beautiful shredded salad is all the different things you can do with it aside from serving it on its own. Use it in tacos, on tostadas, or on sandwiches. It's yummy on Sprouted Garbanzo Burgers (page 155); the shredded apples lend just the right amount of subtle sweetness. The dressing is great on its own as well; try it on sautéed green beans, grilled asparagus, or even potato salads.

# Lime-Bathed Peanut Salad

2 cups unsalted raw peanuts

4 Roma tomatoes, seeded and
chopped

1 large jalapeño chile, seeded
and diced

3/4 cup chopped fresh cilantro

1 tablespoon freshly squeezed
lime juice

1 teaspoon extra-virgin olive oil

1/4 teaspoon fine-grain sea salt

Preheat the oven to 350°F.

Put the peanuts on a rimmed baking sheet and toast for 5
to 10 minutes, shaking the pan once or twice along the way.
If the peanuts have skins, rub them in a clean dish towel to
remove the skins, but don't obsess over this. I actually like
the visual texture you get from having some peanuts with
skins and some without.

Combine the tomatoes, jalapeño, and cilantro in a bowl. In
a separate small bowl, whisk together the lime juice, olive
oil, and salt. Add to the tomato mixture and gently stir to
combine. Just before serving, fold in the peanuts. Taste and
adjust the seasoning with more salt if need be.

*Serves 4 to 6.*

In Mexico City, you can purchase small bags of peanuts that taste as if
they've been misted with salty lime juice. Upon returning from a trip
there, I threw together this quick, zippy salad to emulate their flavor. I
use peanuts, but you could certainly substitute chopped toasted Brazil
nuts or do a mix. If you make the salad ahead of time, keep the peanuts
on the side until just before serving so they don't get soft.

# Hijiki and Edamame Salad
*with Creamy Miso Dressing*

2½ tablespoons dried hijiki

1 pound shelled frozen edamame

Fine-grain sea salt

**CREAMY MISO DRESSING**

¼ cup brown rice vinegar

1½ tablespoons light miso

1 small clove garlic, minced

1 tablespoon unfiltered raw
   honey

½ cup extra-virgin olive oil

Fine-grain sea salt or Toasted
   Nori Salt (page 205)

½ daikon

1 carrot

4 handfuls baby spinach,
   watercress, or arugula

1 (15-ounce) can soybeans,
   drained and rinsed

Rehydrate the hijiki in a bowl of hot water for about 20 minutes. It will double or triple in volume, so start with a large enough bowl. Add the edamame to a large pot of boiling, lightly salted water. After 3 minutes, drain and run under cold water until cold. Salt to taste.

**TO MAKE THE DRESSING**, whisk the rice vinegar, miso, garlic, honey, and olive oil in a small bowl until thick and creamy. Season with big pinches of salt, tasting as you go.

**TO PREPARE THE DAIKON AND CARROT**, use a vegetable peeler to make a pile of long shavings. Then use a chef's knife to cut into thin matchsticks.

Wash the spinach and dry well. In a large bowl, toss the greens with the hijiki, edamame, daikon, carrots, soybeans, and the dressing, a few tablespoons at a time. You want everything to be lightly coated but not drowning. Serve from the big bowl, or turn out onto a nice platter.

*Serves 6.*

A true power salad, delivering a soybean- and seaweed-packed one-two punch. Hijiki contains fourteen times as much calcium as cow's milk, and is rich in iron and protein as well. That being said, the assertive taste of hijiki isn't for everyone. If it is too strong for you, substitute milder-tasting arame or wakame, cut into small strips. Alternatively, you can tame hijiki's fishy flavor by sautéing it in olive oil for a few minutes after it's been rehydrated.

# Sikil Pak

1 habanero chile, stemmed

10 cloves garlic, unpeeled

4 tomatoes

$2^{1}/_{2}$ cups toasted pumpkin seeds
(see page 206)

$^{1}/_{3}$ cup vegetable stock
(page 203)

1 small white onion, finely
chopped

$^{1}/_{4}$ cup finely chopped fresh
cilantro

2 pinches ground cinnamon

$^{1}/_{2}$ teaspoon fine-grain sea salt

Cilantro sprigs, for garnish

In a large, heavy skillet over medium-high heat, char the habanero and garlic cloves until the garlic has patchy dark brown spots and the habanero has char marks all over its skin. Remove from the pan, add the tomatoes, and do the same thing.

Grind the pumpkin seeds into a fine, uniform meal in a food processor. Carefully cut the habanero into quarters and use a paring knife to seed and devein it. If you have a hand blender, combine the habanero, tomatoes, garlic, and stock in a medium bowl and use the hand blender to puree a bit, but leave the mixture semichunky. (Alternatively, use a food processor to do the same thing.) Add the pumpkin seeds and blend again until the consistency is similar to thick mayonnaise; you may need to thin it with a bit of warm water or more stock.

Stir in the onion, cilantro, cinnamon, and salt. Taste and adjust the seasoning if need be. Serve, garnished with cilantro sprigs.

*Makes just over 2 cups.*

In this vibrantly complex Mayan dip, the famously blazing heat of the habanero chile is tempered by tomatoes, a cooling undercurrent of cilantro, and a foundation of pumpkin seeds (pepitas). Serve it with a bowl of fresh Crunchy Topopos (page 94) for dipping. It's even better after a day or two, once the flavors have had a chance to fully meld. The habanero is unbelievably hot, so be careful when you handle it. Try not to touch your eyes or any other sensitive body parts after preparing it.

# Chunky Lentil Soup

1¼ cups green French or black
   beluga lentils, picked over and
   rinsed
2 tablespoons extra-virgin olive oil
1 large yellow onion, chopped
2 cups diced butternut squash
   (¼-inch dice)
1 (28-ounce) can crushed
   tomatoes

1 cup water or vegetable stock
   (page 203)
1 teaspoon fine-grain sea salt
Pinch of smoked paprika or pure
   chile powder (optional)
Torn fresh basil leaves, for garnish
Freshly grated Parmesan cheese,
   for garnish
Good-quality olive oil, for garnish

Bring 5 cups of water to a boil in a large saucepan, add the
lentils, and cook for 20 minutes, or until tender.

Meanwhile, heat the oil in a heavy soup pot over medium
heat, then add the onion and sauté until tender, about 3
minutes. Stir in the squash, tomatoes, and water and continue cooking until the squash is tender, about 10 minutes.
Drain the lentils and stir them in, along with the salt and
smoked paprika. Let the soup return to a gentle simmer,
then taste and adjust the seasoning if need be.

Serve, topped with the basil, Parmesan, and a drizzle of
olive oil.

*Serves 4 to 6.*

As summer starts to wind down and we need more warmth
and sustenance in our food, this earthy, textured pot of
lentils, squash, and tomatoes is a straightforward and
unassuming way to fill the bill. I've tried it with a range of
lentils and have found that peppery French green lentils
and black belugas hold their shape best. Leave a layer of
grated cheese and drizzled olive oil on top of each bowl,
and drag a thick slice of whole-grain artisan bread through
the oozy goodness—either walnut or olive bread would be
a good choice. If you have any smoked paprika or smoky-
flavored chile powder on hand, this would provide a nice
flavor note, but it isn't essential.

# Baby Lima Soup
## *with Chipotle Broth*

1 pound dried baby lima beans,
    picked over and rinsed

10 cups water

1 head garlic, top lobbed off to
    expose the cloves and loose
    skins removed

2 tablespoons clarified butter (see
    page 199)

1 onion, halved top to bottom and
    sliced into thin crescents

1 to 2 chipotles in adobo sauce

2 teaspoons fine-grain sea salt

Squeeze of lime juice (optional)

*My friend Amanda has a job that requires her to seek out the best chaat, thin-crust pizza, and curry in the city. Upon meeting, Amanda and I hit it off immediately and found ourselves combing the aisles of small Mexican grocery stores in San Francisco's Mission District. Wall-to-wall dried beans and chiles were punctuated by towers of steaming, freshly made tortillas. She rattled this recipe off somewhere between the nopales and the posole.*

Look carefully for any pebbles or dirt clumps; baby limas seems to be magnets for dirt. Rinse the beans, then combine them with the water and garlic in a heavy soup pot. You might think putting a whole head of unpeeled garlic in the pot is strange, but just go with it. Bring the beans to an active simmer and cook for 30 to 40 minutes, until just a touch al dente and not mushy or falling apart. Test their doneness by tasting; you really can't tell any other way.

Heat the butter in a heavy skillet over medium-high heat, add the onion, chipotles, and 2 teaspoons of the adobo sauce, and sauté over medium high heat for 3 to 4 minutes, just until the onion starts to soften. You can always add more adobo sauce later for a spicier soup; just don't overdo it on the front end.

Add the salt and the sauté to the pot of beans and simmer gently for about 5 minutes to blend the flavors. The broth should be thin, so add more water if needed. Add more salt and more adobo a bit at a time if the flavors aren't popping. Finish with a squeeze of lime if you like.

*Serves 4 to 6.*

This hearty, comforting soup requires minimal babysitting, and as a bonus, the dainty baby lima beans soften up in about an hour without any presoaking or fuss. You can find chipotles in adobo sauce in the Mexican foods section of most markets. They lend a spicy, smoky, assertive flair that's nicely balanced by the beans and regal reddish gold broth. Try this soup topped with Crunchy Topopos (page 94).

# Creamy Cauliflower Soup
*with Brazil Nut Pesto*

**BRAZIL NUT PESTO**

1/2 cup toasted Brazil nuts
(see page 206)

2 handfuls spinach leaves, stemmed

4 cloves garlic

1/2 cup freshly grated Parmesan
cheese

1/2 cup extra-virgin olive oil

A generous pinch of fine-grain
sea salt

3 tablespoons clarified butter
(see page 199) or extra-virgin
olive oil

2 cloves garlic, chopped

1 large onion, chopped

1 teaspoon red pepper flakes

1 large potato, peeled and
chopped

1 1/2 pounds cauliflower, coarsely
chopped

5 cups vegetable stock (page 203)
or water

1/3 cup heavy cream or Cashew
Cream (page 200)

Fine-grain sea salt

This is a deceptively creamy boil-and-blend soup. The pesto adds vibrant green flair and flavor, but because the soup relies on a somewhat neutral potato and cauliflower base, you can finish it a hundred different ways and it still works. In place of the pesto, consider smoked paprika and toasted croutons made from walnut bread; alternatively, you could sprinkle some Sri Lankan Curry Powder (page 205) on top. Or simply drizzle with toasted nut or seed oil. For a more rustic version, leave the potato unpeeled.

**TO MAKE THE PESTO**, puree all the ingredients in a blender or food processor until smooth. Taste and add more salt if needed to make the rest of the flavors come forward.

Heat the butter in a soup pot over medium-high heat, add the garlic, onion, and red pepper flakes and sauté for 2 or 3 minutes, until translucent. Stir in the potato and cauliflower and cook for another couple of minutes. Add the stock, bring to a simmer, and cook until the vegetables are tender. Remove from the heat and puree thoroughly with a handheld immersion blender. (If you must use a conventional blender, be careful; the hot liquid can burst out the top and make a huge, potentially painful mess. Try leaving the lid slightly ajar to allow steam to escape. Cover the top with a kitchen towel and blend in batches on low speed.) For a silkier texture, push the soup through a sieve or strainer. Stir in the cream and season with salt to taste.

Ladle into individual bowls and finish with a big swirl of the pesto.

*Serves 4 to 6.*

# Garlic Scape Soup

2 tablespoons clarified butter
(see page 199) or extra-virgin
olive oil

2 dozen garlic scapes, flower
buds discarded and green
shoots chopped

3 large russet potatoes, unpeeled
and cut into $1/2$-inch dice

5 cups vegetable stock
(page 203) or water

2 large handfuls spinach leaves,
stemmed

Juice of $1/2$ lemon

$1/2$ teaspoon fine-grain sea salt

Freshly ground black pepper

$1/4$ cup heavy cream (optional)

Chive blossoms, for garnish
(optional)

---

*This simple soup is delicious hot or cold, and even better the day after you make it. Garnish with pretty chive blossoms, sometimes at the market around the same time of year as scapes. When scapes aren't in season, you can make a delicious variation by substituting green onions. Toasted or grilled whole-grain bread rubbed lightly with garlic makes a fine accompaniment.*

Heat the butter in a large saucepan over medium heat, then add the scapes and sauté for 2 minutes. Add the potatoes and stock, cover, and simmer for about 20 minutes, or until the potatoes are cooked through and beginning to break down.

Remove from the heat, add the spinach, and puree using a hand blender. (If you must use a conventional blender, be careful; the hot liquid can burst out the top and make a huge, potentially painful mess. Try leaving the lid slightly ajar to allow steam to escape. Cover the top with a kitchen towel and blend in batches on low speed.) Season with the lemon juice, salt, and a few grinds of pepper. Whisk in the cream for a silkier texture. If the soup tastes flat, add salt a few big pinches at a time until the flavors really pop. Serve garnished with the chive blossoms.

*Serves 4 to 6.*

Scapes are fleeting; don't blink or you'll miss them. For a few short weeks each spring, sometime after the favas and arti-chokes make their debut at the farmers' market, you'll see scapes appear. Look for brilliant, bright green shoots, roughly a foot in length, topped by a small, unopened flower bud. Scapes should be nice and pliable and not overly woody. Smell them and you will know exactly how they taste.

# Chocolate Turtle Bean Tostadas

1 pound black valentine or other black turtle beans, or 5 cups canned black beans, drained and rinsed

2 tablespoons extra-virgin olive oil or clarified butter (see page 199)

2 onions, coarsely chopped

5 cloves garlic, chopped

2 tablespoons pure chile powder

1 tablespoon ground cumin

2 teaspoons ground cinnamon

1 teaspoon ground allspice

4$^{1}/_{2}$ cups water or vegetable stock (page 203)

12 ounces dark beer (stout is a good choice)

2 (4-ounce) chocolate bars, preferably chile-infused, coarsely chopped

Fine-grain sea salt

12 fresh corn tortillas

Crumbled queso fresco or feta cheese, for topping

Chile de Árbol Sauce (page 201), for topping (optional)

Pick over the beans and rinse them well. Soak several hours, or preferably overnight, in enough water to cover the beans by at least 2 inches. Drain and rinse again just before cooking.

Heat the olive oil in a large, heavy pot, then add the onions and garlic and sauté for just a couple of minutes, until the onions start to soften a bit. Add in the chile powder, cumin, cinnamon, and allspice and cook, stirring, for another minute or so, until toasty and fragrant.

Add the beans, water, and beer to the pot and bring to a gentle simmer; if the heat is too low, they'll take forever to cook, but if it's too high, they'll splatter and eventually fall apart. Cook for about an hour (10 minutes if you are using canned), then begin tasting every 10 minutes or so. When the beans are cooked through, remove from the heat and add the chocolate and salt. Taste and adjust the seasoning; if the beans taste a little flat and lackluster, they just need salt. Serve immediately, ladled over fresh corn tortillas and topped with a sprinkling of cheese and a drizzling of chile de árbol sauce.

*Serves 12.*

A simple pot of straightforward beans is a delicious and satisfying thing, but there are times I like my beans to take on a bit more flair. The creamy black turtle bean provides a perfect canvas for a touch of extra spiciness or an undercurrent of unexpected flavors from chocolate and a full-bodied beer. Pair that with a spice-spiked broth, and the result is a pot of beans that is rich, fragrant, and unique. In place of the queso fresco, you can use any similar white, salty cheese, such as cotija or feta. Since it's nearly impossible to find organic Mexican cheeses, you may want to go with feta. If pressed for time, you can certainly use canned black beans. Play around with different kinds and amounts of ground chiles, but be sure to taste as you cautiously add it to the pot. I splurge for the chile-spiked Dagoba Xocolatl here, but any enthusiastically spiced quality chocolate bar will do the trick.

# Grilled Broccoli

*with Lemon and Flaxseeds*

Broccoli
Extra-virgin olive oil
Fine-grain sea salt
Lemon wedges
Ground flaxseeds

Prepare a medium-hot grill—not too hot, as you want the broccoli to cook, not char. If the temperature is right, you should be able to hold your hand a few inches above the grate for 4 or 5 seconds. Cut each head of broccoli into $^1/_4$-inch crosswise sections, about as thick as a pencil, and toss gently with a generous splash of extra-virgin olive oil and a bit of salt. Place the slices in a grill basket and grill for a few minutes with the grill covered to keep moisture in and protect the broccoli from drying out. Flip and grill for 1 or 2 minutes on the other side.

Arrange on a platter and top with a drizzle of olive oil, a generous squeeze of lemon juice, and salt to taste. Finish with a sprinkling of ground flaxseeds.

This hardly counts as a recipe, because when it comes down to it, I'm really just suggesting a different way of cutting broccoli. Slicing these polyphenol powerhouses into pencil-thick cross-sections presents an entirely unique mouth feel—more sleek and flat against the tongue, with an agreeable floret-to-stalk ratio. Grilled, they take on deliciously smoky undertones.

# Golden-Crusted Brussels Sprouts

24 small brussels sprouts

1 tablespoon extra-virgin olive oil, plus more for rubbing

Fine-grain sea salt and freshly ground black pepper

1/3 cup grated cheese of your choice

Trim the stem ends of the brussels sprouts and remove any raggedy outer leaves. Cut in half from stem to top and gently rub each half with olive oil, keeping it intact. Heat the 1 tablespoon olive oil in your largest skillet over medium heat. Don't overheat the skillet, or the outsides of the brussels sprouts will cook too quickly. Place the brussels sprouts in the pan, flat side down, sprinkle with a couple pinches of salt, cover, and cook for about 5 minutes; the bottoms of the sprouts should only show a hint of browning. Cut into or taste one of the sprouts to gauge whether they're tender throughout. If not, cover and cook for a few more minutes.

Once just tender, uncover, turn up the heat, and cook until the flat sides are deep brown and caramelized. Use a metal spatula to toss them once or twice to get some browning on the rounded side. Season with more salt, a few grinds of pepper, and a dusting of grated cheese. While you might be able to get away with keeping a platter of these warm in the oven for a few minutes, they are exponentially tastier if popped in your mouth immediately.

*Serves 4.*

This is the only way to eat brussels sprouts: cut in half and cooked until deliciously tender inside and perfectly brown and crusted on the outside. I look for brussels sprouts that are on the small size and tightly closed. The tiny ones cook through quickly, whereas larger ones tend to brown on the outside long before the insides are done. When the weather is mild, I finish them with a lighter, salty cheese, like Parmesan, but if it's stormy and cold, I opt for a heavier, more melty cheese, like a regular or smoked Gouda.

# Giant Crusty and Creamy White Beans

*with Greens*

.......................................................................................................

$^1$/$_2$ pound medium or large dried
 white beans, cooked (see page
 204)
3 tablespoons clarified butter
 (see page 199) or olive oil
Fine-grain sea salt
1 onion, coarsely chopped
4 cloves garlic, chopped

6 or 7 big leaves chard, preferably
 rainbow chard, leaves cut into
 wide ribbons and 1 or 2 stems
 cut into $^1$/$_2$-inch pieces
Freshly ground black pepper
Extra-virgin olive oil, for drizzling
Freshly grated Parmesan cheese,
 for topping

*For a twist on bruschetta,
serve the beans over
grilled slices of rustic
bread rubbed with a clove
of garlic and a fragrant
extra-virgin olive oil. For a
cold-weather option, omit
the onions and garlic and
instead stir in deeply caramelized onions when you
add the chard.*

Drain the beans, then heat the butter over medium-high heat in the widest skillet you've got. Add the beans to the hot pan in a single layer. If you don't have a big-enough skillet, just do the sauté step in two batches or save the extra beans for another use. Stir to coat the beans with butter, then let them sit long enough to brown on one side, about 3 or 4 minutes, before turning to brown the other side, also about 3 or 4 minutes. The beans should be golden and a bit crunchy on the outside and soft and creamy on the inside. Salt to taste, then add the onion and garlic and cook for 1 or 2 min-utes, until the onion softens. Stir in the chard and cook until just beginning to wilt. Remove from the heat and season to taste with a generous dose of salt and pepper. Drizzle with a bit of top-quality extra-virgin olive oil, and sprinkle with freshly grated Parmesan.

*Serves 6 to 8 as a side dish.*

I get more requests for this recipe than any other. The crisp golden crust on the beans encases a rich and creamy center, creating an irresistibly delicious combination. The greens provide a nutritionally packed accent as well as beautiful color. Plan ahead, as you need to soak the beans overnight. You can even cook them a day or two in advance; drain and store them in the refrigerator until you're ready to use them. I've tried this recipe with canned beans of different varieties, but I always ended up with a mushy pot of bean mash—tasty, but not what we're after. The freshly cooked dried beans maintain their structure much better during sautéing. Giant corona beans, cellini beans, or white cannellini are the best choice here.

When you put a bean or lentil patty on a bun, you run the risk of building a burger that is too dry and bready. The ratio is all out of whack, with not enough ooey-gooeyness to balance the bread and mashed beans. It wasn't until I sat down to write this recipe that I had the revelation I needed: Turn the patty into the bun and stuff *that* with all sorts of good stuff. Problem solved. These make great do-ahead meals, and you can store shaped, ready-to-cook patties in the refrigerator for a week's worth of work lunches. Sprouted garbanzos are becoming more readily available, but if you can't find them, canned or cooked garbanzos will work just fine.

# Sprouted Garbanzo Burgers

2$^1/_2$ cups sprouted garbanzo
   beans (chickpeas) or canned
   garbanzos, drained and rinsed
4 large eggs
$^1/_2$ teaspoon fine-grain sea salt
$^1/_3$ cup chopped fresh cilantro
1 onion, chopped
Grated zest of 1 large lemon

1 cup micro sprouts (try broccoli,
   onion, or alfalfa sprouts),
   chopped
1 cup toasted whole-grain bread
   crumbs (page 206)
1 tablespoon extra-virgin
   olive oil or clarified butter
   (see page 199)

*Filling ideas:*

- *More sprouts (the
  sprouts in the picture
  are ultranutritious
  broccoli sprouts)*

- *Avocado slices*

- *Cipollini onions—
  sweet and just the
  right size*

- *Sliced Roma tomatoes*

- *A sprinkling of
  smoked paprika or
  a drizzle of Chile
  de Árbol Sauce
  (page 201)*

If you are using sprouted garbanzos, steam them until tender, about 10 minutes. If you are using canned beans, jump right in. Combine the garbanzos, eggs, and salt in a food processor and puree until the mixture is the consistency of a very thick, slightly chunky hummus. Pour into a mixing bowl and stir in the cilantro, onion, zest, and sprouts. Add the bread crumbs, stir, and let sit for a couple of minutes so the crumbs can absorb some of the moisture. At this point, you should have a moist mixture that you can easily form into twelve 1$^1/_2$-inch-thick patties. I err on the moist side here, because it makes for a nicely textured burger. You can always add more bread crumbs a bit at a time to firm up the dough if need be. Conversely, a bit of water or more egg can be used to moisten the batter.

Heat the oil in a heavy skillet over medium-low heat, add 4 patties, cover, and cook for 7 to 10 minutes, until the bottoms begin to brown. Turn up the heat if there is no browning after 10 minutes. Flip the patties and cook the second side for 7 minutes, or until golden. Remove from the skillet and cool on a wire rack while you cook the remaining patties. Carefully cut each patty in half, insert your favorite fillings, and enjoy immediately.

*Makes 12 mini burgers.*

# Sushi Bowl with Toasted Nori, Avocado, and Brown Rice

2 cups short-grain brown rice

3 1/2 cups water

2 teaspoons fine-grain sea salt

2 (4-inch) square sheets nori

6 ounces extra-firm tofu

**CITRUS-SOY DRESSING**

Grated zest and juice of 1 orange

Grated zest and juice of 1/2 lemon

2 tablespoons natural cane sugar

2 tablespoons shoyu sauce

2 tablespoons brown rice vinegar

4 green onions, chopped

1 avocado, peeled, pitted, and thinly sliced

3 tablespoons toasted unhulled sesame seeds (see page 206; optional)

A deconstructed sushi roll with a citrus-soy dressing. This is a recipe for those of us who can't be bothered with rolling and shaping rice. I like to experiment with different seasonal vegetables in this recipe; favorites include blanched asparagus tips, edamame, and oven-roasted or sautéed sliced mushrooms.

Rinse and drain the rice two or three times. Combine the rice, water, and salt in a heavy saucepan and bring to a boil over high heat. Lower the heat, cover, and simmer gently until the water is absorbed, about 45 minutes.

Toast the nori in a preheated 300°F oven or a medium-hot skillet for a few minutes. Crumble or chop coarsely.

Drain the tofu and pat it dry. Cut the block of tofu lengthwise through the middle to make four 1/4- to 1/2-inch sheets of tofu. Two at a time, cook in a dry nonstick or well seasoned skillet over medium-high heat for a few minutes until browned on one side. Flip gently, then continue cooking for another minute or so, until the tofu is firm, golden, and bouncy. Let cool enough to handle, then cut crosswise into matchsticks. Repeat with the remaining sheets.

**TO MAKE THE DRESSING**, set the zests aside. Combine the orange juice, lemon juice, and sugar in a small saucepan and bring to a gentle boil. Cook for 1 or 2 minutes, then add the shoyu and vinegar. Return to a gentle boil and cook another 1 or 2 minutes, until slightly thickened. Remove from the heat and stir in the zests.

When the rice is done, stir in 1/3 cup of the dressing and add more to taste. Scoop the rice into individual bowls and top with the toasted nori, green onions, tofu, avocado slices, and a sprinkling of sesame seeds.

*Serves 4 to 6.*

# chapter five

# Use Natural
# Sweeteners

# USE NATURAL SWEETENERS

So, you've picked up a few of the more naturally produced sweeteners outlined in the pantry chapter, and now you want to know what to do with them. The recipes in this chapter will show you how to use blackstrap molasses in conjunction with whole-grain flours to make sticky-sweet spice loaves (page 189) and how to re-create a version of your favorite minty Girl Scout cookie minus the white sugar and trans fats. Preserves and fruit spreads are notorious for using astronomical amounts of sugar and high-fructose corn syrup, so I'll give you a recipe for making one from market-fresh figs sweetened with honey (page 170). And if you're looking for a sweetly delectable quencher, check out the recipe for white sangria spiked with agave nectar instead of simple syrup (page 169).

It is important to understand the roles that sweeteners play in cooking and baking before you embark on a journey like this. Beyond sweetness, they also bring moistness and tenderness to baked goods. They can lend body and volume to batters and doughs and often form the foundation for icings, frosting, and glazes. In the case of caramel corn, they act as the binding agent, and it is sugar that gives you the dense, delicious crumb of your favorite coffee cake and the golden crust on a big muffin top. As a decorative element, granulated sugars can add a finishing texture to everything from a truffle to the rim of a cocktail glass, and this sort of use is one of the best ways to explore some of the more expensive artisanal sugars that are beginning to hit the market.

Overconsumption of sugar is a major problem in this country, and some folks have totally given in to their sweet tooth, often without realizing it. But if you cut out processed foods, with their deluge of highly processed sweeteners, you should feel little guilt about indulging in sweets in moderation.

The following section will outline the sweeteners I most commonly use, along with descriptions of how I like to use them. For an outline of what to look for in the grocery or natural foods store, see "Sweeteners" (page 17).

AGAVE NECTAR won't seize up in cold drinks the way honey does, and because it dissolves quickly in cold ingredients, it's particularly useful for cocktails and smoothies. Like honey, it is sweeter than table sugar

($1^1/_4$ times as sweet), so as you start experimenting with agave nectar, use roughly $3/_4$ cup nectar for every 1 cup of white sugar in the original recipe. You will also need to reduce other liquids a bit and, in recipes that require baking, scale back oven temperatures by 25°F to prevent overbrowning.

BLACKSTRAP MOLASSES has a strong, distinct, slightly bitter and acidic flavor that can overpower other ingredients if you aren't careful. You don't really want to trade in all the sugar in a recipe for molasses. A blend is often the best bet, substituting a quarter, and working up to half the sugar called for. Use $1^1/_4$ cups molasses for 1 cup of sugar. You'll need to scale back the liquid by $1/_4$ to $1/_3$ cup and lower the oven temperature by 25°F to prevent overbrowning. Because it's more acidic than sugar, add a teaspoon of baking soda for each cup of molasses you use; this will help temper the acidity. Also, keep in mind that it will lend a dark color to baked goods.

I use BROWN RICE SYRUP as the coating for caramel corn or as a sweet medium to which I add other granulated sweeteners and flavors, allowing its beautiful texture to remain intact. Keep in mind that it's only about half as sweet as white granulated sugar. Sometimes, I spike up its sweetness by combining it with natural cane sugar or maple syrup, just to give it a bit more oomph.

Anyone who has tasted a zahidi date knows just how intensely sweet and flavorful dates can be, making them well suited to sweetening other foods. But you can't treat DATE SUGAR, made from ground dates, like other granulated sweeteners. It doesn't dissolve in liquid, and tends to burn easily. It is also quite pricey. I like to highlight its sweet, rich flavor in spreads and fillings, sprinkle it on oatmeal, or dust it on top of cakes and cookies immediately after they emerge from a hot oven.

Fine-grain NATURAL CANE SUGAR is adaptable, delicious, fragrant, and easy to work with. It can typically be substituted for granulated sugar on a one-to-one basis, or if you are particularly nervous about ruining your favorite recipes, start with a blend. Experiment with different brands and note the differences in flavor, color, and texture. Refer to the pantry chapter for an in-depth explanation about what to look for when you are shopping for cane sugar, or see Sources for details on a few recommended brands. If you can't find anything that fits these descriptions, I would opt for Florida Crystals, a readily available sugar made from organic sugarcane. Because most natural cane sugars are somewhat dark, I also turn to Florida Crystals when I'm after a granulated sweetener that is lighter in color as in the Ginger-Amaranth Shortbread on page 177.

HONEY has the highest sugar content of all the natural sweeteners. It lends flavor and moisture to baked goods, and I especially enjoy experimenting with different varieties of honey in gelatos and ice creams, driz-

zling them over cheeses, and using them as a base for salad dressings and dipping sauces. For those of you who are allergy prone, consuming honey made by bees in your immediate area can help defuse allergies. When replacing sugar with honey, start by substituting $^1/_2$ cup honey for each cup white granulated sugar. Reduce the liquid in the recipe by $^1/_4$ cup, increase the baking soda by $^1/_4$ teaspoon, and decrease the oven temperature by 25°F. Keep in mind that it's easy to overdo it when sweetening with honey, so use a light touch.

MAPLE SUGAR has less sweetening power than white granulated sugar, but because many recipes are written overly sweet, substituting cup for cup is a good place to start. You might want to start by using it as an accent sweetener. For a real treat, use it in place of half the sugar in the Sticky Teff-Kissed Spice Loaves (page 189), or sprinkle it over your morning oatmeal.

Use MAPLE SYRUP to sweeten warm comfort foods like oatmeal, quick bread batter mixes, winter squash soups, corn bread batter, French toast, billowy Belgian waffles, and the Wild Rice Flour Pancakes on page 43. It's less sweet than granulated sugar, and as with most of the other liquid sweeteners, I wouldn't recommend substituting it for all of the granulated sugar in a baked recipe; start with a percentage. Baked goods sweetened with maple syrup tend to be more dense, moist, dark, and heavy. This is good thing if you want a hearty loaf cake, but not if you're after a cloudlike angel food masterpiece. It takes $1\frac{1}{2}$ cups of maple syrup to equal the sweetness in 1 cup of white sugar. For every 1 cup of syrup used, decrease the amount of liquid by $\frac{1}{4}$ cup or increase the flour by $\frac{1}{4}$ cup. Also, add $\frac{1}{4}$ teaspoon of baking soda for each cup of maple syrup used, to counterbalance the increased acidity in the syrup.

# White Sangria

*with Agave Nectar and Drunken Peaches*

2 or 3 peaches, peeled, pitted, and cut into eighths

3 cups seedless grapes of mixed colors, halved

$1/3$ cup agave nectar

2 (750–ml) bottles sauvignon blanc

$1/2$ cup apricot brandy

1 (1–liter) bottle sparkling water

Combine the peaches, grapes, agave nectar, wine, and brandy in a 1-gallon jug. Stir gently so the fruit doesn't break up, then chill in the refrigerator for a few hours or, even better, overnight.

Serve in tall glasses, making sure each has a nice assortment of the wine-soaked fruit; top each with a generous splash of sparkling water.

*Makes 1 large pitcher, enough to serve 6 to 8.*

This spritzy white wine sangria is accented with peach slices. Choose peaches that are lusciously flavorful but not overly ripe, or they'll disintegrate into the sangria. The agave nectar is clean–tasting and mild–flavored enough that it sweetens without distracting from the other ingredients.

# Fig Spread with Black Pepper and Toasted Sesame Seeds

1¹/₂ pounds ripe fresh black Mission figs, stemmed and cut into ¹/₄-inch dice

¹/₄ cup freshly squeezed lemon juice

¹/₃ cup honey

¹/₄ teaspoon freshly ground black pepper, plus more as needed

¹/₄ cup toasted unhulled sesame seeds (see page 206)

Toss the chopped figs and lemon juice together in a large bowl. Stir in the honey and black pepper and set aside for 10 minutes. The figs will start to break down and get soupy. Pour the fig mixture in to a large, heavy pot over medium heat and bring to a slow, gurgling boil. Cook, stirring constantly, until the figs start to reduce and thicken, about 10 to 15 minutes. Stir in the sesame seeds and remove from the heat. Let the spread sit for 5 minutes, taste, and add more pepper to taste if needed.

This spread may be canned as you would other jams, but it keeps well for up to a week in the refrigerator.

*Makes 3 cups.*

This beautiful jewel-toned preserve is versatile enough to start the day on a slice of walnut toast or end it as part of a cheese plate. Sweetened with honey and slightly chunky, it's a welcome change from overly sweet high-fructose-corn-syrup-based commercial preserves.

# Thin Mint Cookies

1 cup unsalted butter, at room
    temperature
1 cup powdered sugar
1 teaspoon pure vanilla extract
1 cup nonalkalized cocoa powder
1 egg white

$3/4$ teaspoon fine–grain sea salt
$1^1/_2$ cups whole–wheat pastry flour
1 pound semisweet chocolate,
    chopped
$1^1/_2$ teaspoons peppermint oil, or
    $1/_2$ to $1^1/_2$ teaspoons peppermint
    extract, plus more as needed

Preheat the oven to 350°F, position the racks in the middle
of the oven, and line 2 baking sheets with parchment paper.

Using a stand mixer or handheld mixer, cream the butter
until light and fluffy. Add the powdered sugar and cream
some more, scraping the sides of the bowl a time or two. Stir
in the vanilla extract, cocoa powder, egg white, and salt and
mix until the cocoa powder is integrated and the batter is
smooth and creamy and has the consistency of thick frosting.
Add the flour and mix just until the batter is no longer dusty
looking. It might still be a bit crumbly, and that's okay; if you
overmix, you'll and end up with tough cookies.

Turn the dough out onto a floured work surface, gather it
into a ball, and knead it just once or twice to bring it together
into a smooth mass. Place the dough in a large plastic bag
and flatten it into a disk roughly 1 inch thick. Put the dough
in the freezer for 20 minutes to chill.

A remix of a classic, minus the shortening and trans–fats from partially hydrogenated vegetable oils. Just good old–fashioned butter, cocoa, vanilla, sugar, chocolate, whole–grain flour, and peppermint turned into delicious, thin–minty goodness.
Wholesome Sweeteners brand offers a good organic powdered sugar, and for a real
treat, try Dagoba's cacao powder.

Remove the dough from the freezer and roll it out quite thin, about $1/6$ inch thick. But don't roll it too thin, or the cookies will crumble when you dunk them in the chocolate coating. You may find it easiest to roll it out between two sheets of plastic. Stamp out cookies using a $1^{1/2}$ inch cutter, place on the prepared baking sheets, and bake for 10 minutes, or until they smell of deep warm chocolate, with toasty overtones. (You'll have to trust your nose on this one!) Remove from the oven and cool completely on wire racks.

Meanwhile, make the chocolate coating. Slowly melt the chocolate, stirring occasionally, in a double boiler (you can cobble together a makeshift one by placing a metal bowl over a saucepan of gently simmering water). When the chocolate is glossy and smooth, remove from the heat and whisk in the peppermint oil a little at a time. Alternatively, you can use extract added in $1/2$-teaspoon increments. If you think the chocolate needs a bit more peppermint kick, keep adding more peppermint oil a few drops at a time, but taste as you go.

Cover the baking sheets with clean parchment paper. Coat the cookies one at a time, lowering each into the chocolate and gently turning with a fork until fully coated. Using the fork, lift the cookie out of the chocolate and allow any extra chocolate to drizzle back into the pan. Aim for a thin, even coating of chocolate. Gently set the cookies on the prepared baking sheets, then transfer to the refrigerator or freezer to set. Although they will set at room temperature, it takes much longer.

*Makes 2 to 3 dozen cookies.*

# Spiced Caramel Corn

1 teaspoon clarified butter (see
  page 199)
$^1/_2$ cup unpopped popcorn
$^1/_2$ cup brown rice syrup
$^1/_2$ cup maple syrup
$^1/_2$ teaspoon ground cinnamon

$^1/_2$ teaspoon freshly grated
  nutmeg
$^1/_2$ teaspoon pure chile powder
1 teaspoon fine-grain sea salt
1 cup mixed toasted nuts and
  seeds (see page 206)

*You can also make popcorn balls with this recipe—something kids love to do. Instead of cooling the coated popcorn on a baking sheet, let it sit until cool enough to handle, then mold into balls or whatever shape you wish using clean, damp hands.*

Heat the butter in a large, heavy pot over high heat. Add the popcorn and cover with a lid. When the corn starts popping, shake the pan constantly to prevent the kernels from burning. When the rate of popping falls off dramatically, immediately remove from the heat and remove the lid.

Line a baking sheet with parchment paper. In another large pot, stir together the syrups, cinnamon, nutmeg, chile powder, and salt and bring to a boil over medium heat. Resist stirring with a spoon; instead, carefully swirl the mixture for 5 minutes, until actively bubbling, starting to reduce, and deeply fragrant. Stir in the nuts, seeds, and popcorn and mix gently until everything is well coated. Turn out onto the prepared baking sheet, gently spread it out, and allow to cool.

*Serves 6.*

An addictive blend of sweetness, saltiness, and spiciness envelops clusters of freshly popped corn and nuts. The maple syrup and brown rice syrup pair nicely with warming spices, but feel free to experiment with different blends of spices and ingredients: Try Indian curry powder and shredded coconut; chunks of crystallized ginger and sesame seeds; or walnuts and dried cherries finished with a dusting of maple sugar. Any nuts and seeds will work in this recipe, so use your favorites, and don't overlook more unusual choices, such as pumpkin seeds, pistachios, or chopped macadamias.

# Ginger-Amaranth Shortbread

1¹/₂ cups white whole–wheat flour

¹/₂ cup amaranth flour

³/₄ teaspoon fine–grain sea salt

1 tablespoon ground ginger

1 cup unsalted butter, at room
   temperature

²/₃ cup natural cane sugar

¹/₃ cup minced crystallized ginger

Combine the flours, salt, and ground ginger in a small bowl
and whisk to combine.

In a separate large bowl or stand mixer, cream the butter
until light and fluffy. Add the sugar and mix again, then
add the dry ingredients and mix until just combined and
crumbly. Stir in the crystallized ginger by hand and turn the
dough out onto a floured work surface. Knead the dough
just once or twice to bring it together, then gather it into a
ball and flatten into a disk 1 inch thick. Wrap in plastic wrap
and refrigerate for 15 minutes.

Preheat the oven to 350°F and line a baking sheet with
parchment paper. Roll the dough out to a ¹/₄-inch thickness
on a lightly floured work surface. Cut into whatever shapes
you desire, imprint a design using a cookie stamp if you
like, and place on the prepared baking sheet. Freeze for 10
minutes, then bake for about 10 minutes, or until the cookies are beginning to brown on the bottom. The baking time
will vary depending on the size of the cookies, taking less
for smaller cookies.

*Makes about 2 dozen*
*1-inch square cookies.*

In this whole–grain, double–ginger shortbread, I use Florida Crystals sugar rather
than less–refined natural cane sugars to keep the color lighter. This brand of sugar
is made from organic sugarcane, but it's filtered during processing. The result is a
sugar that isn't as rich in minerals and flavor as other natural sugars, but its pale
color makes it ideal when you don't want the sugar to darken whatever it is that
you're cooking. If you don't mind a darker color, use a less refined brown natural
cane sugar instead.

# Dairyless Chocolate Mousse

$^1/_2$ cup chocolate soy milk

$1^1/_2$ cups semisweet chocolate
  chips

12 ounces silken soft tofu

$^1/_4$ cup amaretto (almond
  liqueur)

$^1/_4$ teaspoon pure almond extract

Fine-grain sea salt

*For a fun presentation (reminiscent of softserve deliciousness), pipe the mousse into individual serving cups by using a makeshift pastry bag. Snip the corner of a ziplock plastic bag and spoon the mousse into the bag. Squeeze out all the air as you push the mousse into the snipped corner, then pipe the mousse in a circular motion into cordial cups, parfait glasses, or even large shot glasses.*

Pour the milk into a small saucepan and slowly bring to a simmer. Remove it from the heat and set aside to let cool a bit.

Slowly melt the chocolate, stirring occasionally, in a double boiler (you can cobble together a makeshift one by placing a metal bowl over a saucepan of gently simmering water).

Add the warm soy milk and silken tofu to the melted chocolate chips. Puree with a hand blender or transfer to a blender or food processor and process until silky smooth. Stir in the amaretto, almond extract, and a generous pinch of sea salt. Taste and adjust the flavoring, adding a bit more extract if needed.

Chill in a large serving bowl or individual bowls for at least $1^1/_2$ hours—the longer the better. The mousse will set up nicely as it cools.

*Makes 6 servings.*

Rich and decadent, this almond-spiked chocolate mousse happens to be dairy free and vegan. If you want to be more adventurous, instead of the almond flavorings, infuse the simmering milk with fresh spearmint, generous pinches of ground chile, or anything that goes well with chocolate. This mousse also makes a nice butter-free frosting. For the soy milk, I recommend Vitasoy Rich Chocolate Soy Milk. Tropical Source and Sunspire both make excellent all-natural, dairy-free chocolate chips. *Don't* substitute carob chips for the chocolate; the flavor just isn't comparable.

# Double-Chocolate Pistachio Biscotti

1 1/4 cups whole-wheat pastry
flour

3/4 cup white or regular whole-
wheat flour

1/3 cup oat flour

1/3 cup wheat germ

1/2 teaspoon fine-grain sea salt

1 teaspoon aluminum-free
baking powder

1/2 cup nonalkalized cocoa
powder

6 tablespoons unsalted butter, at
room temperature

3/4 cup natural cane sugar

3 large eggs

1/2 cup chopped pistachios

3/4 cup good-quality semisweet
chocolate chips

These double-chocolate biscotti made with whole-grain flours and peppered with bright green pistachios are perfect for dunking. Once you get the hang of it, feel free to swap in different types of nuts, dried fruits, crystallized ginger, or your favorite chocolate-friendly spices.

Preheat the oven to 325°F and line a baking sheet with parchment paper.

Combine the flours, wheat germ, salt, baking powder, and cocoa powder in a bowl and whisk to combine.

In a separate large bowl or stand mixer, cream the butter until light and fluffy. Add the sugar and mix again, then stir in the eggs one at a time and mix until well combined, scraping down the sides of the bowl a couple of times to distribute the eggs evenly. Stir in the dry ingredients and mix just until the dough becomes stiff and the flour is incorporated, then stir in the pistachios and chocolate chips. The dough should be on the stiff side but easy to work with.

Turn the dough out onto the prepared baking sheet. Flatten and mold the dough into an inch-thick flattened log roughly 4 inches wide by 10 or 12 inches long. It doesn't have to be perfect—rustic looking biscotti taste just as good. Bake for 25 minutes, until firm and richly fragrant.

Remove from the oven and lower the oven temperature to 300°F. Allow the now-baked dough to cool for about 10 minutes so it won't crumble when you cut it. Slice the loaf into individual biscotti roughly 3/4 inch thick. I like to cut diagonally across the loaf so that I end up with a range of sizes. Lay the slices flat on a baking sheet and bake until dry and firm, another 30 minutes, or so. Cool on a wire rack.

*Makes about 12 big biscotti.*

# Red Quinoa–Walnut Cookies

2$\frac{1}{2}$ cups whole–wheat pastry flour

1 teaspoon baking soda

1 teaspoon aluminum–free baking powder

$\frac{3}{4}$ teaspoon fine–grain sea salt

1 cup unsalted butter, at room temperature

2 cups natural cane sugar

3 large eggs

3 teaspoons pure vanilla extract

2 cups cooked red quinoa (see page 55)

$\frac{3}{4}$ cup chopped toasted walnuts (see page 206)

1 cup rolled oats

Preheat the oven to 375°F, position the racks in the upper half of the oven, and line 2 baking sheets with parchment paper.

Combine the flour, baking soda, baking powder, and salt in a bowl and whisk to combine.

In a separate large bowl or stand mixer, cream the butter until light and fluffy, then beat in the sugar. Mix in the eggs one at a time, incorporating each fully before adding the next and scraping down the sides of the bowl a few times. Sir in the vanilla until evenly incorporated. Add the flour mixture in about 4 increments, stirring between each addition. At this point, you should have a moist, uniform dough. Stir in the quinoa, walnuts, and oats and mix only until the quinoa is evenly distributed.

Drop 2 tablespoons of the dough on the prepared baking sheets for each cookie. Bake for 10 or 12 minutes, until golden on both top and bottom.

*Makes 2 to 3 dozen medium-large cookies.*

These cookies are a great way to use up leftover quinoa. Red quinoa lends a nice color, but any color will work. This makes a big batch, so you may want to bake a dozen and shape and freeze the rest to bake as needed.

# Mesquite Chocolate Chip Cookies

2<sup>1</sup>/<sub>2</sub> cups whole-wheat pastry flour

1 cup mesquite flour, sifted if
   clumpy

1 teaspoon baking soda

1 teaspoon aluminum-free baking
   powder

<sup>3</sup>/<sub>4</sub> teaspoon fine-grain sea salt

1 cup unsalted butter, at room
   temperature

2 cups natural cane sugar

3 large eggs

1 tablespoon pure vanilla extract

2 cups rolled oats

2 cups semisweet chocolate chips

Preheat the oven to 375°F, position the racks in the upper half of the oven, and line 2 baking sheets with parchment paper.

Whisk together the flours, baking soda, baking powder, and salt in a bowl. Set aside.

In a large bowl or stand mixer, beat the butter until light and fluffy, then beat in the sugar until of a consistency like thick frosting. Beat in the eggs one at a time, incorporating each fully before adding the next and scraping down the sides of the bowl a few times. Stir in the vanilla until evenly incorporated. Add the dry ingredients in 3 increments, stirring between each addition. At this point, you should have a moist, uniformly brown dough. Stir in the oats and chocolate chips by hand, mixing only until evenly distributed.

Drop 2 tablespoons of dough for each cookie onto the prepared baking sheets 2 inches apart and bake for about 10 minutes, until golden on both top and bottom. Don't overbake these; if anything, underbake them. Cool on wire racks.

*Makes 2 to 3 dozen chunky, medium-large cookies.*

Chances are you're new to mesquite flour, a wonderful, fragrant flour made from the ground-up pods of the mesquite tree. It has a slightly sweet and chocolaty flavor, with a touch of malt and smokiness. Look for mesquite flour that is fragrant, powdery, and finely ground. If you can't find it locally, see Sources for mail-order suppliers. If you don't have any mesquite flour, substitute 1 cup whole-wheat pastry flour in its place; your cookies will still turn out oozy, chewy, and delicious.

# Raspberry Curd Swirl Cake

1¹/₂ cups whole-wheat pastry flour

1¹/₂ teaspoons aluminum-free baking powder

³/₄ teaspoon fine-grain sea salt

³/₄ cup unsalted butter, at room temperature

1¹/₂ cups natural cane sugar

3 large eggs

1 teaspoon pure vanilla extract

³/₄ cup fresh raspberries, halved (optional)

³/₄ cup raspberry curd

Powdered sugar, for dusting

Softly whipped cream, for serving (optional)

Preheat the oven to 350°F and position the racks in the middle of the oven. Choose your cake pan and butter it generously.

Combine the flour, baking powder, and salt in a small bowl and whisk to combine.

*This cake will work in a variety of pans. I typically use an 8 by 4-inch loaf pan, but a 9- or 10-inch spring-form should work as well. Just keep an eye on your cooking time and adjust accordingly.*

In a large bowl, use a stand mixer or handheld mixer to beat the butter until smooth and creamy. Add the sugar and beat again. Scrape down the sides of the mixing bowl once or twice during the process so you end up with a nice, even, creamy blend. Beat in the eggs one at a time, incorporating each fully before adding the next and scraping down the sides of the bowl a few times. If you don't beat well enough at this stage, you'll end up with little butter-sugar flecks throughout the batter in the end. Stir in the vanilla until evenly incorporated. Add the dry ingredients and gently fold them in by hand just until the last of the flour barely disappears; don't overmix. Fold in the berries.

Scoop half of the cake batter into the prepared pan. It's pretty thick, so you may need to spread it around a bit with the back of a spoon. Now spread about half of the curd a over the batter, staying clear of the sides of the pan. Add the rest of the batter and smooth the top until level, then plop big spoonfuls of the remaining curd on top of the cake (again staying clear of the sides of the pan). Drag a butter knife

*(continued on page 188)*

This bright, berry-streaked loaf cake pairs perfectly with a lazy day, a bit of sunshine, and a rolling green lawn, making it the perfect picnic cake. Moist, dense, and sliceable, this travel-friendly cake has a surprise burst of flavor that comes by way of a beautifully colorful curd swirl. Look for curds (also known as fruit butters) that contain all-natural ingredients next to the jams and jellies at your local gourmet grocer or see Sources for online suppliers. Change the type of curd you use with the seasons: Try cranberry curd in autumn, citrus in winter, and raspberry in summer.

through the curd in a loop-de-loop motion so the cake batter swirls with the curd to create a marbled effect.

Bake for 50 to 60 minutes, or until the cake bounces back a bit when you push the top of it with your finger. The baking time will vary depending on pan size and shape. The cake should be very moist, so don't overcook it; trust your eyes, nose, and instinct. Let cool in the pan. Slice and serve at room temperature, dusted with a bit of powdered sugar and with a side of softly whipped cream if you like.

*Serves 12 picnickers.*

This recipe yields a pair of sweet, crusty-topped, sticky-centered spice loaves—one to keep, one to give to a neighbor or friend. When I'm trying to outdo myself, I'll stir in $1/2$ cup of chopped crystallized ginger just before pouring the batter into pans. If you can't find teff flour, mesquite flour complements the spices in this cake beautifully. If you have a hard time finding both teff and mesquite flour, use all whole-wheat pastry flour (3 cups total); the cakes will still be delicious.

# Sticky Teff-Kissed Spice Loaves

2 cups whole-wheat pastry flour

1 cup brown teff flour

1¹/₂ teaspoons baking soda

¹/₂ teaspoon fine-grain sea salt

2 teaspoons ground ginger

1 tablespoon ground cinnamon

¹/₂ teaspoon ground allspice

¹/₄ teaspoon ground cloves

1 cup unsalted butter

¹/₂ cup water

³/₄ cup blackstrap molasses

³/₄ cup honey

1 cup natural cane sugar

3 large eggs, at room
   temperature

¹/₂ cup milk

1-inch piece fresh ginger, peeled
   and grated

Freshly whipped cream, for
   topping

Preheat the oven to 325°F and position the racks in the middle of the oven. Butter and flour two 8 by 4-inch loaf pans, tapping out any extra flour.

Combine the flours, baking soda, salt, ground ginger, cinnamon, allspice, and cloves and whisk to combine.

*These cakes keep beautifully in the refrigerator for up to a week. I've also found they freeze remarkably well double-bagged in plastic with the air pressed out.*

Combine the butter, water, molasses, honey, and sugar in a small saucepan over medium heat. Cook, stirring, until well-blended. Pour into a large bowl and let cool until it isn't hot on your tongue when you're sneaking a taste. Whisk in the eggs one at a time and then the milk. Switch to a rubber spatula and fold in the dry ingredients in 3 increments. You might have a few lumps, but resist overmixing. Fold in the grated ginger.

Pour the batter into the prepared pans and bake for 50 to 60 minutes, or until loosely set in the center. Don't overbake or you'll lose much of the signature stickiness. Let cool in the pan. Slice and serve with a big dollop of whipped cream.

*Makes 2 spice loaves.*

Panna cotta (Italian for "cooked cream") is deceptively simple to prepare. A short list of ingredients, a few minutes of active cooking time,
and you have an elegant yet not overly fussy dessert. Both the panna
cotta and the berry coulis can be made a day or two ahead of time.

If you can't find agar flakes, look for agar powder. I recommend the
organic Florida Crystals sugar, rather than darker natural sugars, so the
panna cotta will have its traditional pale color. You can puree the berries for a smoother, more refined texture, but I think the rustic texture
of barely mashed berries is a nice complement to the smoothness of the
panna cotta. Chopped mangoes and toasted coconut would of course be
another delicious topping here.

# Coconut Panna Cotta
*with Summer Berry Coulis*

**COCONUT PANNA COTTA**

1 (14-ounce) can coconut milk

1 1/4 cups milk

1/3 cup light-colored natural
  cane sugar

1 1/2 tablespoons agar flakes, or
  3/4 teaspoon agar powder

**SUMMER BERRY COULIS**

1 cup fresh raspberries

1 cup fresh blackberries

1/4 cup natural cane sugar (less if
  the berries are super ripe)

Juice of 1/2 lemon

12 Animal Crackers (page 189),
  for garnish (optional)

*Agar is a powerful, neutral-tasting gelling agent made from seaweed. Unlike other thickeners, agar will set at room temperature. When using it in other recipes, keep in mind that acids will weaken its gelling power. If you're firming an acidic liquid, increase the amount of agar. It is also worth noting that the enzymes in certain raw fruits can inhibit agar's ability to gel—figs, mangoes, papayas, and kiwi for starters. Cooked, they aren't a problem.*

**TO MAKE THE PANNA COTTA**, lightly oil 6 ramekins and set aside. Place the coconut milk, milk, sugar, and agar flakes in a pan. Stir, then let rest for 10 minutes to allow the agar to soften and start to dissolve; this is particularly important if you're using flakes. Very slowly, bring the ingredients to a gentle simmer and continue to simmer for a few minutes, until the agar is incorporated. If it doesn't completely dissolve, pour the mixture through a strainer, pushing the undissolved agar through as well. Pour into the prepared ramekins and chill until set, about 1 hour.

**TO MAKE THE COULIS**, combine the berries, sugar, and lemon juice in a small saucepan, bring to a simmer, then remove from the heat. Mash the berries a bit, then chill.

Serve the panna cotta either in the ramekins or turned out carefully onto small plates; top with the berry coulis and garnish with animal crackers, if you like.

*Serves 6.*

You can make these thin, crispy, light (and sweet) crackers from cookie cutters of any shape, size, or theme. I've found chia seeds make nice eyes, but only if you have the patience to drop them into place with tweezers. Be vigilante once the crackers are in the oven; they go from undercooked to burnt in a flash, so you need to watch them closely. Use a mix of whatever seeds you like. I like to use the sesame-heavy bunch of seeds always left at the bottom of the container of my favorite seed-crusted crackers.

# Peanut Butter Krispy Treats

$^3/_4$ cup smooth unsalted peanut
    butter

$^3/_4$ cup maple syrup

1 scant teaspoon fine-grain sea salt

$2^1/_2$ teaspoons agar flakes

4 cups unsweetened crisp brown
    rice cereal

Combine the peanut butter, maple syrup, salt, and agar flakes in a large saucepan over low heat and stir constantly until smooth, hot, melted, and bubbling just a bit. Add the cereal and stir until well coated. Transfer to an 8 by 8-inch baking dish and press into place with a wooden spoon or a piece of waxed paper. Refrigerate until completely cool, then cut into 2 by $1^1/_2$-inch rectangles with a sharp knife.

*Makes 20 snack-sized treats.*

This twist on the classic crispy rice treat is nuttier and more flavorful than the standard version, which uses commercial marshmallows and rice cereal. Once you get the method down, you can start playing around with different nut butters, different puffed cereals, and add-ins like dried fruit, nuts, and seeds. Be sure to buy crisped brown rice cereal and not puffed rice cereal, for the best results.

# Animal Crackers

<sup>1</sup>/<sub>4</sub> cup natural cane sugar

1<sup>1</sup>/<sub>2</sub> teaspoons ground ginger

<sup>1</sup>/<sub>4</sub> teaspoon fine-grain sea salt

1 egg

1 tiny splash of heavy cream

1 package of 6-inch wonton
  wrappers

<sup>1</sup>/<sub>4</sub> cup mixed seeds (such as
  poppy seeds, sesame seeds,
  and caraway)

Animal-shaped cookie cutters

Preheat the oven to 350°F, position the racks in the middle
of the oven, and line a couple of baking sheets with parchment paper.

In a small bowl, combine the sugar, ginger, and salt. In a
separate bowl, whisk the egg and cream together. Cut the
wonton wrappers into various animal shapes using the
cookie cutters. Brush the wontons with a thin glaze of the
egg mixture. Sprinkle each with seeds, and then a generous
dusting of the sugar mixture.

Move the wontons into a single layer on the baking sheets
and bake until the wontons are golden and crisp, 5 to 8
minutes. Don't let them burn!

*Makes 2 dozen crackers.*

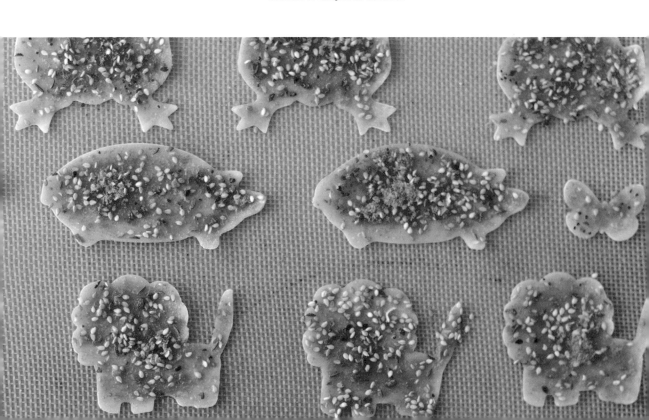

Ricas AGUAS
FRESCAS

PIÑA

ORCHATA
JAMAICA

LIMON
SANDIA
TAMARINDO

de Frutas Naturales

Basic Recipes
and Techniques

Certain basic recipes and techniques are so essential in a natural foods kitchen that you'll use them repeatedly on a day-to-day basis. I've featured some of the basics I turn to often here. The tofu-based mayo on page 200 is not used in this book, but is so useful that I couldn't bring myself to leave it out.

# Clarified Butter

Many oils are damaged before you ever purchase them, whether during processing or during storage and shipping. If they aren't damaged at purchase time, many are damaged soon thereafter with high-temperature cooking methods like frying or baking. (For more details, see "Oils and Fats," page 11.) Clarified butter can stand up to high-temperature cooking better than most other natural, unrefined cooking fats and oils because it's comprised mostly of saturated fat and isn't high in delicate essential fatty acids. You can purchase organic clarified butter from many grocery and natural foods stores, but it is easy and more economical to make your own.

Clarified butter is unsalted butter that has had the milk solids removed. (The milk solids are the components that will eventually burn or break down at high heat.) The end product is a pure, glorious, golden butter fat with a smoking point around 375°F. It doesn't have the same flavor profile as regular butter; it's lighter in flavor, with a nice kiss of buttery depth.

*You can control the nutti-ness and overall intensity of clarified butter by varying how long you cook the butter before removing it from the milk solids. If you want a darker, nuttier clarified butter, cook the butter longer. The solids will become aromatic and toasty and will impart a beautiful hazelnut color to the butter. In Indian cooking, this form of clarified butter is known as ghee.*

1 pound unsalted butter

Gently heat the butter in a small saucepan over medium-low heat. The butter will separate into three layers. Foam will appear on the surface of the butter, the milk solids will migrate to the bottom of the pan, and the clarified butter will float between the two. This should only take a few minutes. Skim the foamy layer off with a spoon and discard. Next, carefully pour the golden middle layer into a jar, leaving the milk solids at the bottom. (Discard the solids, too.)

Clarified butter will keep for a month or two at room temperature and a month or so longer when refrigerated.

*Makes 1 1/2 cups.*

# Egg-Free, Dairy-Free Mayonnaise

Use this on sandwiches, potato salads, or anywhere else you'd use commercial mayo. You can infuse or blend it with different flavors, just as you would regular mayonnaise or aioli.

8 ounces extra-firm tofu
2 tablespoons freshly squeezed lemon juice
3 tablespoons extra-virgin olive oil
1/2 teaspoon fine-grain sea salt
1/2 teaspoon dijon mustard
Pinch of cayenne pepper

Wrap the tofu in a few paper towels, then press and gently squeeze to release excess moisture. Combine the tofu, lemon juice, olive oil, salt, mustard, and cayenne in a food processor and blend until very smooth, 30 seconds or so. Thin with warm water to reach desired consistency.

*Makes 1 1/2 cups.*

# Cashew Cream

As much as I enjoy top-quality, local organic heavy cream, there are times when I want the spirit of heavy cream without the decadence. This nut-based alternative has become one of my favorite substitutions. You can infuse it with other flavors, or use it as a simple base anywhere you'd use regular cream. Puree it with chives in the spring, chile puree and roasted garlic in the fall, citrus zest in the winter—endless variations are possible. It makes a good replacement for heavy cream in pasta sauces.

1 1/2 cups raw cashews
1 1/2 cups water, plus more as needed
2 1/2 teaspoons nutritional yeast
1 1/2 teaspoons fine-grain sea salt
Squeeze of lemon juice

Soak the cashews in a small bowl of warm water for 20 or 30 minutes to soften them up, which makes for a smoother, silkier cream. Drain and add the 1 1/2 cups water, the nutritional yeast, and salt. Puree with a hand blender or food processor until smooth, pourable, and of a creamlike consistency; this may take 2 or 3 minutes of steady blending, so be patient. You may need to add additional water, a few tablespoons at a time, to achieve the right consistency. This cream tends to thicken over time, and is absorbed into pasta quickly, so err on the thin side. Season the cream with a squeeze of lemon juice, then stir, taste, and add a bit of additional salt if needed.

*Makes about 2 cups.*

# Chile de Árbol Sauce

Drizzle this wonderful rich and vibrant sauce on everything from savory crepes and cheesy quesadillas to frittatas, roasted vegelables, and burritos. It's one of my favorite condiments, so I make a batch once a week or so and keep it in the refrigerator at all times.

6 tablespoons clarified butter (page 199) or extra-virgin olive oil

8 chiles de árbol, stemmed

20 cloves garlic, unpeeled

2 cups vegetable stock (page 203)

$1/2$ teaspoon fine-grain sea salt

$1/3$ cup heavy cream or Cashew Cream (page 200; optional)

Have a large bowl of very hot water on hand. Heat 3 tablespoons of the butter in a large, heavy skillet over medium heat, then add the chiles. Toast for about 1 minute, or until fragrant. Transfer the chiles to the bowl of hot water and add the garlic to the pan. Cook, turning each clove once or twice, until the peels start browning and the insides soften, about 8 minutes.

Soak the chiles until soft and pliable, 20 to 30 minutes (if the water starts to cool, drain and refill with more hot water). Meanwhile, peel the garlic. Drain the chiles, slice lengthwise and remove the seeds. Puree the chiles, garlic, and stock with a hand blender or food processor. If you are in a rush and don't mind a bit of extra heat, you can cut back on the soaking time and purée the whole chiles.

In the same skillet in which you cooked the garlic, heat the remaining 3 tablespoons butter over medium-high heat, then add the chile puree. It should really sizzle when it hits the pan. Stir regularly for 10 minutes, or until reduced by about half. Remove from the heat and stir in the salt. It is quite strong like this, and you may want to temper it by stirring in a bit of heavy cream.

*Makes about 1 cup.*

# Bright Red Tomato Sauce

A light-textured and vibrant-tasting red sauce perfect on everything from pastas and thin-crust pizzas to lasagnas and panini. For a more rustic version, substitute fire-roasted crushed tomatoes. A sprinkle of lemon zest added at the end is a nice addition, lending an unexpected hint of flavor. Use ladled over the Gnocchi alla Romana (page 105) and the Grilled Polenta-Style Teff Wedges (page 58).

2 tablespoons extra-virgin olive oil

$1^{1}/2$ teaspoons red pepper flakes

3 cloves garlic, minced

1 teaspoon fine-grain sea salt

1 (28-ounce) can crushed tomatoes

Combine the olive oil, pepper flakes, garlic, and salt in a saucepan. Bring to a simmer over medium-high heat and sauté for 2 to 3 minutes, or until the garlic begins to take on the slightest bit of color. Stir in the tomatoes, return to a simmer, and cook for 5 minutes. Remove from the heat and season with more salt to taste.

*Makes 3 cups.*

# Honey-Based Simple Syrup

This is a twist on traditional simple syrup. Honey doesn't integrate into cold ingredients or drinks very well unless you thin it out. Use in mixed drinks when you want a bit of sweetness with honey overtones.

$1/2$ cup very hot water
$1^1/2$ cups mild-flavored honey

Pour the hot water over the honey and mix until incorporated. Store in a clean jar at room temperature.

*Makes 2 cups.*

# Mesquite Syrup

A bit of mesquite flour adds a surprise twist to maple syrup. It adds a unique taste to everyday oatmeal, and pairs nicely with the Wild Rice Flour Pancakes on page 43. Brush it on tofu before it hits the grill or winter vegetables before or after roasting.

$2/3$ cup maple syrup
$1^1/2$ tablespoons mesquite flour, sifted

Warm the maple syrup in a small saucepan. Add a few tablespoons of the syrup to the mesquite flour and stir to form a paste. Add the paste to the rest of the warm syrup and stir until well incorporated.

*Makes $2/3$ cup.*

# All-Natural Baking Powder

Most commercial baking powders contain aluminum, something most of us don't need any extra exposure to. If you have difficulty locating an aluminum-free baking powder, you can make it yourself. This is a single-acting baking powder that activates and begin to fizz when it hits liquid. Be sure your oven is preheated and your baking pans are ready before you mix the batter.

1 part baking soda
2 parts cream of tartar
2 parts arrowroot

Mix everything together and store in an airtight container. This baking powder should last up to a month. To see if it is still active, drop a teaspoonful into a glass of hot water. If it bubbles vigorously, the powder is still active.

# Roasted Red Bell Peppers

Whether cut into strips, blended into a puree, or stuffed whole, the options for roasted red peppers are endless. I use them regularly in Muhammara (page 102), a delicious spread for slathering on all types of foods. When I'm too lazy to roast peppers, I seek out good-quality jarred roasted peppers packed in water (and their own juices); they can typically be substituted with no problem. Puree a few into your next batch of hummus or blend into a paste with roasted garlic cloves and salt for a flavor-packed sandwich or pizza spread.

4 red bell peppers

Preheat the oven to 400°F and position a rack in the middle. Place the peppers on their sides and not touching on a rimmed baking sheet. Roast, rotating once or twice along the way, until they bubble, char, and begin to collapse, about 45 minutes. Don't be afraid of black spots.

Remove from the oven and immediately transfer to a glass bowl and cover with plastic wrap. Uncover after 10 minutes, then use your fingers to peel the skins off. Remove the seeds and cores.

# Vegetable Stock

For those of you who have minimal patience for long-simmering stocks, this is a quick-cooking, mild-tasting alternative. For the times when home-made stock isn't an option, there are delicious all-natural bouillon cubes available (see Sources). I use them quite often with delicious results, but the key is choosing the right brand and flavor.

2 tablespoons extra-virgin olive oil
2 onions, cut into eigths
2 shallots, quartered
1 garlic clove, smashed
2 celery stalks, chopped
A few sprigs thyme
$1^1/_2$ teaspoons fine-grain sea salt
2 quarts water

Heat the oil in a large stockpot over medium-high heat. Add the onions, shallots, garlic, celery, and thyme. Sauté for 5 minutes and then add the salt and water. Bring to a boil, then lower the heat and simmer for at least 30 minutes or up to 1 hour. Strain and use in soups, risottos, and sauces.

*Makes 2 quarts.*

# A Simple Pot of Beans

There are as many impassioned theories on how to cook beans as there are days in the year. After much experimentation, I've developed a few theories of my own about how to attain the premium pot. For starters, anytime you're trying out a new type of bean, I recommend forgoing fancy preparations. Cook them simply, using the instructions below, and take some time to really taste and explore that bean for its unique flavor, texture, and personality. Soon, you'll start to develop a sense of what you can do with each to highlight its uniqueness. Some lend themselves to a delicious pureed soup, while others are best enjoyed whole. One might pair nicely with a stronger broth or sauce, and another might be perfect on its own with a drizzling of olive oil and a dusting of grated cheese. Cooking beans with a stamp-sized piece of kombu seaweed for every cup or so of beans, makes them easier to digest.

Start by picking through the beans carefully, looking for small pebbles or clumps of dirt. Then rinse thoroughly.

If you have time to soak the beans, do so— either overnight or starting early the morning of the day you want to cook them. Although soaking isn't a mandatory step, it will speed your cooking time and impart a beautiful fullness to each bean that you don't always get when you skip the soaking step. Soaking becomes more essential with older beans that have been in storage longer. It is also credited with leaching out some of the indigestible sugars credited with causing gas.

Place 1 pound of dried beans in a large, heavy pot and add enough water to cover by a few inches. Leave overnight or at least 5 hours.

After soaking, drain the beans and discard the soaking water, then add fresh water in an amount roughly double or triple the volume of the beans. Chop half an onion and toss it in (or add a combination of chopped aromatic vegetables, like onions, celery, and carrots). Bring the pot to a simmer and cook until tender. Depending on the type of bean and its freshness, cooking time can range from 45 minutes to a couple of hours. Sample regularly to gauge doneness.

Season with salt in the last 15 to 20 minutes of cooking time, when the beans are nearly ready. This gives them enough time to start absorbing some of the salt but won't cause the skin of the bean to seize up and resist absorption of water, which results in tough beans. It's not a good idea to add salt or a salty stock earlier in the cooking process. Enjoy your pot of beans on their own, or incorporate them into your favorite bean-friendly recipe.

*Makes about 2$^1/_2$ cups.*

# Sri Lankan Curry Powder

Deeply fragrant and with a touch of heat from the red chiles, this Sri Lankan curry blend is a beautiful yellowish orange from a generous hit of antioxidant-rich turmeric. Use it as a spice rub, on nuts or popcorn, as a seasoning for roasted vegetables, or to add color and liveliness to your favorite recipes. See the Curried Tofu Scramble (page 90).

3 to 4 dried red chiles, such as cayenne
1 tablespoon coriander seeds
1 tablespoon cumin seeds
1 tablespoon fennel seeds
1 (1-inch) piece cinnamon
$1/2$ teaspoon cardamom seeds
$1/2$ teaspoon whole cloves
1 tablespoon ground turmeric

Toast the chiles, coriander, cumin, fennel, cinnamon, cardamom, and cloves in a dry skillet over medium heat until fragrant, about 1 or 2 minutes. Stir constantly so the spices don't burn. Remove from the heat and grind until fine in a spice grinder or mortar. Stir in the turmeric and store in an airtight jar in a dark place.

*Makes $1/3$ cup.*

# Toasted Nori Salt

A deep green, sea-scented alternative to standard salt. Use it as a seasoning in and on everything from spring rolls and salads to edamame and popcorn.

Nori sheets
Fine-grain sea salt

Toast the nori for a few minutes in a preheated 300°F oven or a medium-hot skillet until slightly fragrant and crumbles easily. Remove, break into smaller pieces, and grind in a mortar or spice grinder until of the same consistency as the salt you are using. Mix the toasted nori and an equal amount of salt and store in an airtight container.

# Toasting Nuts and Seeds

I generally toast flatter nuts and seeds in a skillet—pine nuts, sesame seeds, and those that have been chopped. Rounder nuts, such as walnuts, hazelnuts, and peanuts, go in the oven so heat can wrap all the way around them.

**IN A SKILLET:** Place nuts or seeds in a single layer in a large, heavy skillet over medium heat. Toss them around every few minutes until fragrant and toasty. Don't walk away, or if you must, set a timer for just a couple of minutes so you don't forget; I've learned the hard way after burning countless batches of pine nuts.

**IN THE OVEN:** Preheat the oven to 350°F. Place the nuts on a rimmed baking sheet so they don't roll off and toast until they start to darken and get fragrant. Toasting time varies depending on the nut, but this usually takes just a few minutes. The nuts toward the edges tend to brown faster, so stir the nuts or give the pan a shake a time or two during baking.

# Whole-Grain Bread Crumbs

Play around with different types of breads here—whole wheat, walnut, oat bread, and so on. You can make bread crumbs from any of them. Bake a big batch and store part in the freezer so you'll always have some on hand. If you don't want to make your own, there are some good, natural whole-wheat bread crumbs available these days. Natural whole-wheat versions of the crunchier, bigger-grained Japanese panko are now available, too (see Sources).

Day-or-two old whole-grain bread, crusts removed

Pulse the bread (in batches if necessary) in a food processor until you have a textured crumb. I sift out the fine sandy crumbs that collect at the bottom of the processor, which leaves just the good stuff, but this is an extra step you don't have to take.

# SOURCES

A short list of the sources to explore when stocking your natural foods pantry.

## ALTER ECO

WWW.ALTERECO-USA.COM

This company offers an array of fair trade products, including a granulated sweetener that's moist and delicious, with whispers of vanilla. This beautiful golden-brown sugar sets the bar for other sugar producers. I suspect (and hope) they will have wider in-store distribution by the time this book comes out. If you can't find it locally, you can order it in bulk from Amazon; get a few friends to go in on a case. Organic and fair trade certified.

## ANSON MILLS

WWW.ANSONMILLS.COM

Offers organic heirloom grains milled into beautiful flours and meals.

## BOB'S RED MILL

WWW.BOBSREDMILL.COM

Purveyors of a fantastic line of flours, including white whole-wheat flour, teff flour, amaranth flour, and rice flour, with many organic products.

## CHRISTOPHER BROOKES DISTINCTIVE FOODS

WWW.CBDF.COM/ELIZABETHANPANTRY.HTML

All-natural curds, preserves, toppings, and condiments.

## DAGOBA

WWW.DAGOBACHOCOLATES.COM

Among their many delicious offerings is non-alkalized, organic cocoa powder.

## EDEN ORGANICS

WWW.EDENFOODS.COM

A supporter of organic agriculture since 1968, Eden offers many macrobiotic products, including sea vegetables, miso, barley malt syrup, sea salts, and more.

## ESSENTIAL LIVING FOODS

WWW.ESSENTIALLIVINGFOODS.COM

A wide variety of unusual wild-crafted and organic products, including mesquite flour.

## FLAVORGANICS

WWW.FLAVORGANICS.COM

Organic pure extracts.

## FLORIDA CRYSTALS

WWW.FLORIDACRYSTALS.COM

If you can't find less-refined cane sugar, look for Florida Crystals organic sugar. Widely available at natural foods stores, it falls somewhere in the middle of the sugar spectrum: It's organic and less processed than white granulated sugar, so it maintains some flavor and is free of preservatives and artificial ingredients. You can use it just as you would white sugar.

## IAN'S NATURAL FOODS

WWW.IANSNATURALFOODS.COM

One of the few sources for whole-wheat panko (Japanese bread crumbs).

## MADHAVE HONEY COMPANY

WWW.MADHAVAHONEY.COM/AGAVE.HTM

A good source of organic, kosher 100 percent agave nectar.

## MARANATHA

WWW.MARANATHANUTBUTTERS.COM

Offers a variety of nut butters, including organic peanut butter made with 100 percent organic dry-roasted peanuts and no sweeteners. Delicious!

## ORGANIC PLANET

WWW.GREAT-EASTERN-SUN.COM

It's hard to find whole-grain Asian-style noodles; most are made with enriched flours. Organic Planet makes a great line of organic, non-GMO, heirloom-grain noodles. I use their noodles quite often for curries (see page 107).

## RANCHO GORDO

WWW.RANCHOGORDO.COM

Specializing in New World foods, my friend Steve Sando offers a fantastic line of heirloom beans, dried posole, grains, wild rice, and herbs.

## RAPUNZEL

WWW.RAPUNZEL.COM

Has a nice unrefined, unbleached powdered sugar made from evaporated organic sugarcane juice. It is a buff color and tastes a bit of molasses. They also make my favorite vegetable bouillon cubes, which come in two versions: with and without sea salt. I usually use the salted version at about half strength to better control the salt levels in my recipes; typically 1 cube to 4 or 5 cups of water.

## SAN PEDRO MESQUITE COMPANY

HTTP://SHOP.SPMESQUITE.COM

Sells mesquite flour.

## SPECTRUM ORGANICS

WWW.SPECTRUMORGANICS.COM

Expeller-pressed cooking oils, many available organic and unrefined.

## THE TEFF COMPANY

WWW.TEFFCO.COM

Mail-order teff grain and flour, both brown and ivory, from a teff grower in Idaho.

## WHOLESOME SWEETENERS

WWW.WHOLESOMESWEETENERS.COM

Sugars and sweeteners produced without bleaching agents or bone char. Their organic blackstrap molasses is particularly good. A good source for agave nectar, too.

## ZINGERMAN'S

WWW.ZINGERMANS.COM

Wild rice, pomegranate molasses, spices, vinegars, and more, from carefully chosen sources.

# INDEX